NUMBER 907

THE ENGLISH EXPERIENCE

ITS RECORD IN EARLY PRINTED BOOKS
PUBLISHED IN FACSIMILE

THOMAS BECON

THE DEMAUNDES
OF THE
HOLY SCRIPTURE

LONDON, 1577

WALTER J. JOHNSON, INC.
THEATRUM ORBIS TERRARUM, LTD.
AMSTERDAM 1979 NORWOOD, N.J.

The publishers acknowledge their gratitude to
the Syndics of Cambridge University Library
for their permission to reproduce the
the Library's copy, classmark: Syn.8.57.109,
and to the Curators of the Bodleian Library,
Oxford, to reproduce pp. C_1r, B_3r, B_5r, B_6v,
F_3r-F_5r from the Library's copy,
shelfmark: 1.g.119.

S.T.C. No 1718

Collation: A-G^8.

Published in 1979 by

Theatrum Orbis Terrarum, Ltd.
Keizersgracht 526, Amsterdam

&

Walter J. Johnson, Inc.
355 Chestnut Street
Norwood, New Jersey
07648

Printed in the Netherlands

ISBN 90 221 0907 0

Library of Congress Catalog Card Number
79-84087

¶ The Demaundes of holy Scripture, with answeres to the same,

wherein are defined, and declared the
cheefe, and principall poyntes of Christian
doctrine : very profitable for the right
vnderstanding of holy Scriptures:
made by T. Becon, and
dravven out of his
great vvorkes.

(∴)

Matth. 7.

Aske, and it shall be geuen you. Seeke, and ve shall
finde. Knocke, and it shall be opened vnto you.

Iames. 1.

If any of you lacke vvysdome, let him aske of hym,
that geueth it: euen God, vvhich geueth to al men
indifferently, and casteth no man in the teeth, and
it shall be geuen him. But let him aske in faith, and
vvauer not : for he that doubteth, is like a vvaue of
the Sea, vvhich is tost of the vvindes, and caryed
vvith violence. Neither let that man thinke, that
he shall receiue any thing of the Lorde. A vvaue-
ring minded man, is vnstable in all his vvayes.

AT LONDON,
Printed by Iohn Day.
1577.
Cum Priuilegio.

I. *Peter.* 3.

Be ready alvvayes to geue ansvvere to euery man
that asketh you a reason of the hope that is in
you, and that vvith meekenesse and feare, hauing a
good conscience, that vvhere as they backbite you
as euyll dooers, they may be ashamed, that falsely
accuse your good conuersation in Christe.

Apocalips. 3.

Thou sayest, I am riche and encreased vvith goods,
and haue neede of nothing, & knovvest not hovve
thou art vvretched and miserable, and poore, and
blind, & naked. I counsell thee to bye of me, gold
tryed in thefyre, that thou mayest be riche : and
vvhite rayment, that thou mayest be clothed, that
thy filthy nakednesse do not appeare: and annoint
thyne eyes vvith eye salue that thou mayst see.

¶ To the godly, and right
woorshipfull Senate, the Mayre and
his brethren of Sandwich in Kent.
Thomas Becon vvysheth long
life, continuall health, and
prosperous felicitie.

O oft as I consider the blessed
state of your tovvne, vvhereof God
by his deuine prouidence and vnsear-
cheable counsell, hath made you rulers vnder the Queenes Maiestie, our
Soueraigne liege Lady: I am entirely prouoked and
stirred vp to geue most entire thankes, to the Prince
of Princesses, and Lorde of Lordes, that mighty
G O D of Hostes, for his so great and singuler be-
nifites, so bounteously and largely poured vpon
you, and other the inhabitauntes of your tovvne.
For I doo not vvell knovve, yf any thing may any
vvhere be found, meete to beautifie a common
vveale, that iustly may be counted to lacke in you,
so plentifully hath G O D poured his blessinges
vpon you. VVho is able to expresse, vvhat a good-
ly ornamente, precious ievvell, and noble ouche,
Christian doctrine is, to a Christian common
vveale? The sage and prudent Philosophers, and o-
ther vvyse and expert men of this vvorlde, iudged
these common vveales most blessed, happy, and fortunate, most noble, beautifull, and florishing, vvhere
the Princes and Rulers thereof, vvere eyther Philosophers, or studious of Philosophie. But hovv much
is that common vveale to be counted happy and
blessed, vvhere not humaine Philosophie, vvherthat

A.ij.

vve respect naturall, or morall, but diuine Philosophie, brought from the hie Heauens, by him vvhich
is the vvysdome of the father, prospereth, florisheth,
triumpheth: vvhere also not vaine and curious Philosophers, but true, faithfull, and godly Philosophers raigne, and beare rule? VVhatoeuer the Philosophers taught, although neuer so much enforced
vvith sugred eloquence, probable reasons, and ap-
parent argumentes, it vvas the fruite of the earth,
and of mans braine: but that vvhiche Christe deliuered vnto vs, came out of the bosome of his Father, so that looke hovve much the noble Heauens
surmount & passe the vile & base Earth in higth, &
indignitie: so much, and incomparable vvyse more,
doth the heauenly Philosophie, vvhereof the holy
Ghost alone is the aucthour, exceedeth the earthy
Philosophie, vvhereof man is the deuiser. He that
cómeth from an high, sayth that blessed Iohn Bap-
tist, is aboue all. He that is of the earth, is earthy, &
speaketh of the earth. He that commeth from Heauen, is aboue all, and vvhat he hath seene and heard,
that he testifieth: and no man receiueth his testimonie. He that hath receiued his testimonie, hath set
to his seale, that G O D is true. For he vvhom
G O D hath sent, speaketh the vvoordes of God.
VVhat other thing is this diuine Philosophie, vvher
of vve novve speake, then the holy vvoord of God?
And vvhat other are these faithfull and godly Philosophers, then the true preachers and professours
of the sacred Scriptures? All these are to be founde
among you plentifully. The Christian Philosophie,
I meane the vvoord of G O D, raigneth, ruleth,
and triumpheth among you, so that according vn-

Iohn. 3.

to it, all things are ordered among you in that your Tovvne. In other places, this diuine and Chriſtian Philoſophie, is counted hereſie, nevve learnyng, ſtraunge doctrine, the mother of errours, the cauſe of rebellion, ſedition, inſurrection, &c. and the plaine ſubuertion of common vveales: but vvith you, & that moſt iuſtly it is reperted & taken for the alone trueth, for the ancient doctrine of the Patriarches, Prophets, and Apoſtles, for the mother of all godlynes and vertue, for the onely & alone cauſe of vnitie, concord, quietneſſe, amitie, obedience, and for the alone ſtay, vpholding, and maintenance of all Chriſtean, and vvell ordred common vveales, ſo that vvhere this is not, there is a Chaos, and plaine confuſion of thinges. This holy vvoord of GOD among you, ſvvimmeth not in your lippes only, but it alſo ſhineth in your lyfe and conuerſation, vnto the good example of all them that are conuerſant vvith you. By this vvoord, according to the commaundement of GOD geuen to Ioſua, ye do not only frame your ovvne life, but ye alſo gouerne your Tovvne, and iudge al cauſes that come before you, as a rule, from the vvhich it is not lavvfull for you by any meanes to depart. Of this vvoord ye reuerently talke, commune, conferre, ſing, and haue continuall meditation, as your chiefe ioy and comfort. This vvoord is vnto you, that noble treaſure Matth. 13. hydde in the Feelde, the vvhiche a man found and hydde, and for ioy thereof, goeth and ſelleth al that he hath, and byeth the Feelde. This vvoord is to you more ſvveete, then the Hony, or the Hony Combe, and more precious then Gold, or Precious ſtone. And as this moſt bleſſed and holy vvoorde dooth occupie the principall and highest place among you: so haue you both godly profeſſors, and faithfull preachers of the ſame, vnto the great ioy aud ſingular comfort of all the inhabitauntes of your Tovvne. For as there can not be a greater ievvell in a Chriſtian common vveale, then an earueſt faythfull, and conſtant preacher of the Lordes vvorde: ſo can there not be a greater plague among any people, then vvhen they haue raigning ouer them blind guides, dumme dogges, vvicked vvolues hypocriticall hyrelinges, popiſhe Prophetes, vvhich feede them not vvith the pure VVheate of Gods vvoord, but vvith the VVoormevvód of mens try-ſling traditions, and vvith the ſovvre leauen of the Papiſticall Phariſees, as Salomon ſayth: VVhen the preaching of Gods vvoord ſayleth, the people pe-riſhe, and come to nought. Veryly as there is not a greater bleſſing geuen of G O D to any nacion, then the gift of his vvoord: ſo I knovve, not yf a greater curſſe from G O D can be caſt vppon any people, then vvhen the vvoord of G O D, and the true preaching thereof is taken avvay from them, as theſe vvoordes of G O D ſpoken by the pro-phete, doo manifeſtly declare. Beholde, the tyme commeth (ſayth the Lorde G O D) that I ſhall ſend an hunger into the earth, not the hunger of bread, nor the thyrſt of vvater, but an hunger to heare the vvoord of the L O R D: ſo that they ſhal goe from the one ſea to the other, yea from the North, to the Eaſt, runnyng about to ſeeke the vvoord of the Lorde, and ſhall not finde it. In this behalſe therfore, are ye the inhabitauntes of Sand-vviche greatly bleſſed of the Lord our God, vvhich hath not onely very richely geuen you his vvoorde to be preached, taught, and read among you, but also hartes to receaue and beleeue the same, as yf vve reade of Lydia, vvhose hart (sayth blessed Luke, the Lorde opened, that shee attended to the thinges vvhich Paul spake. Out of this your feruent zeale and burnyng loue tovvard this diuine and heauenly Philosophie, many godly and Christen fruites of Gods spirite, haue issued and plentifully come foorth, as brotherly concord, and vnfained amitie among your selues, not your selues onely, but also among all the inhabitauntes of your Tovvne, so that all contention, strife, debate, discord, emnitie, variaunce, tumultes, quarelles, lavvynges.&c. banished, and auoyded: beneuolence, loue, concord, agreement, vnitie, amitie, freendship gentlenesse, humanitie, and vvhat oeuer maketh vnto the bond of peace, ruleth and raigneth among you, vvhich godly vnitie and concord dooth so euidently declare you to be of God, as nothing more. this shall all men knovve, that ye are my Disciples (sayth Christe) yf one of you loue an other. As discord bringeth al thinges to hauocke: so dooth concord conserue, keepe in good order, and make to increase vvhat so euer is good and profitable to a common vveale, or to any part thercof. As Salustius sayth: By concord, small thinges encrease and grovve: but by discorde, mighty and great thinges decay, and come to nought. It vvas very vvittely and learnedly ansvveared of Terence, vvhen the noble Senate of the most noble Romanes demaunded of him after the destruction of Carthage, vvhat he thought to be the cause of the subucrtion if so

margin: Actes.16.

margin: In Iohn.13.

ample, populus, and florishing citie, vvhether the puissaunce of the Romans, vvhose force seemed to be incomparable, or the feeblenesse of the Carthaginenses not being able to resist, No, sayth he, neyther your valiance, nor our vvant of puissance, vvas the subuersion of our citie, but the discorde of the Citizens. The mightiest fortresse, and strongest Bulvvarcke, that eyther Citie or Tovvne can haue, is the concord of Citizens, vvithout the vvhich, all puissaunce, all force, all vvytte, al pollicie, all castels, all martiall armonies are vayne, and vnprofitable, verely in this behalfe, are ye also greatly blessed of God, vvhich both in godly & vvorldly affaires, are of one mind, & of one meaning, vvithout al dissencion among you. O blessed fruite of Gods spirite. Moreouer, hovve idlenesse that chiefe maistres of vices all, vtterly exiled, and banished out of your Tovvne? No man liueth there idlely. All degrees of persons are godly, vertuously, and profitably occupied, euery man according to his vocacion and calling. All studye to be quiet, and to meddle vvith theyr ovvne businesse, and to vvorke vvith theyr ovvne hands, that they may not only eate theyr ovvne breade according to the commanndement of God, but also through those their laboures haue vvhereof they may geue vnto such as haue neede, as Saint Iohn saith, he that hath tvvo coates, let him geue one to him that hath none. And he that hath meate, let him doo likevvise. Certes diligent, and vertuous trauaile, vpholdeth the Citie: but idle and sluggysh hands, roote vp the foundacions thereof.

Furthermore, vvho can yenough prayse and sufficiently

Luke. .3.

uiently commende your studious, carefulnesse, and painefull trauaile, in making prouision for the poore members of Christe, vvhith haue not of them selues, vvhereof to liue? Verely yee haue a fatherly care for your poore, that none of them should vvant. Ye count their lacke, your ovvne lack: neyther are ye lesse moued vvith theyr miseries, then yf ye your selfs vvere touched vvith the same, according to this saying of Saint Iohn. He that hath the substance of this vvoorld, and seeth his brother haue neede, anb shutteth vp his compassion from him, hovy dvvelleth the loue of God in him? Vnmercifulnesse tovvard the poore, vvas one of the chiefe causes, vvhy that florishing and to much vvealthy Citie Sodome (as the Prophet teacheth) vvas destroyed vvith fire, an brimstone from heauen. Verely euen so contraryvvise, vvhere the vvorkes of mercie are diligently practised vpon the poore, there is the blessing of God, conseruation of the Tovvne, or Citie, encrease of goodes, and fortunate successe in all honest and godly trauayles, as Salomon sayth: He that geueth to the poore, shall not vvant. He that lendeth to the Lorde, that shevveth mercie to the poore, and it be recompenced him to the vttermost, as our Sauiour Christe sayth: Geue, and it shalbe geuen vnto you: good measure, and pressed dovvne, and shaken togeather, and runnyng ouer, shall men geue into your bosomes: For he that geueth but a cuppe of cold vvater for Christes sake, shall not loose his revvard. Yf thou vvylt breake thy bread to the hungry, sayth GOD by the Prophete, and leade the needy vvayfaring man into thy house, & couer the naked man,

1. Ioan. 3.

Ezech. 16.

Luke. 6.

Esay. 58.

A v. and

and not turne avvay thy face from the poore : thy lyght shall breake foorth as the mornyng , and thy health florishe right shortly: yea, thy righteousnesse shal goe before thee, and the glory of the Lord shal embrace thee . Then yf thou callest, the Lord shall aunsvvere thee : yf thon cryest , he shall say : Here I am. O blessed is the man, sayth the Psalmographe, that considereth the poore and needy : the Lorde shall deliuer him in the time of trouble. The Lorde shall preserue him and keepe him aliue, that he may be blessed vpon earth, and not be deliuered into the vvyll of his enimies . The Lorde shall comfort him, vvhen he lyeth sicke vpon his bedde , yea and make his bedde in his sieknesse.

Agayne, vvhat shall I speake of your gentle and louyng enterteynement of strangers and forreners, vvhich for the testemony of Christes most glorious Gospell, and for the quietnesse of theyr conscience, that they may the more freely serue. G O D vvith a pure mind, are not only content to suffer vnvvorthy banishment vvith the losse of their goodes, but also day and nyght to labour vvith their ovvne handes for their liuing, that they may be no burden to any man. These most vvyllyngly and gladly ye admit, receauc, and embrace, cherishe, entertayne, and comfort . These ye lodge & place among you, not as strangers , but as Citizens , not as forreners, but as your dearely beloued Christian brothers: for vvhom also ye are no lesse carefull then for your selues, that nothing be lacking vnto them, but that they may haue sufficiently of all good and necessariethinges. This is the true hospitalitie, I meane, the gentle enterteynement of godly straungers , vviche

are

are afflicted for the wordes sake. Of these speaketh
GOD on this manner: Yf a straunger soiourne Exod.22.
with thee in your land, ye shall not vexe him . But Leuit.19.
the stranger that dwelleth with you, shalbe as one
of your selues, and thou shalt loue him as thy selfe.
Of these speaketh Christ on this wyse: I was har- Matth. 25.
bourlesse, and ye tooke me in. Of these speaketh
Saint Paul thus : Distribute to the necessitie of the Romans.12.
Saintes. Be redy to harbour . Agayne , Be not for- Hebru. 13.
getfull to lodge straungers : for thereby haue diuers Gene.19.
men lodged. Angels vnwares Of these speaketh S. 1.Peter.4.
Peter on this sort: Be ye harberors one to another
without grudging. Of these speaketh Saint Iohn Leuit.19.
on this manner. Thou dooest faythfully, whatsoe- and.23.
uer thou dooest to the brethren, and to the straun- Deut.24.
gers. Of these, G O D in his lawes geueth a speci- 1.Tim.4.
all charge both to the riche men , and also to the Titus.1.
Byshoppes and spirituall Pastors of his congregation, that they should see to them, and make prouo-
sion for them, that they lacke nothing. Highly in
Gods fauour must the godly straungers be, seeing
G O D geueth to his people so great charge ouer
them. VVho therefore can othervvyse, then highly
commend the louing gentlenesse, and gentle loue,
the bountous liberalitie , and liberall bountie,
which ye shevve to the poore scattered member
of Christe? These be vvoorthy sruites of the Gospell. These vvoorkes shevve, that ye haue not receiued the grace of God in vayne : and that ye be
not of the company of those Gospellers, vvhiche
vvith their mouth professe G O D, but vvith their
deedes deny him, being abominable, and disobedi-
ent, and vnapt vnto euery good vvoorke. Such professours Titus.1.

feſſors or rather peruerſers of the Goſpell , are like
to that Sonne, vvhich promiſed his father to vvork
in his Vineyard , and vvrought nothing at all. Yea
they are, as Saint Iude termeth them in his Epiſtle,
cloudes vvithout vvater , trees vvithout ſruite , ra-
ging vvaues of the ſea , foming out their ovvne
shame, vvandring ſtarres, to vvhome is reſerued the
miſt of darkneſſe for euer, fleſhely, hauing no ſpirit.
&c . and in deede like to thoſe fiue fooliſh Virgins,
vvhich had Lampes, but in theyr Lampes no Oyle,
and not vnlike to the Figge tree vvithout ſruite,
vvhich Chriſt curſed ſor her barrenneſſe.

   But God(right vvorshipful and dearely beloued)
hath geuen you an other minde, and grafted in you
a better ſpirite , that yee do not only knovve God,
but alſo earneſtly labour to do his holy and bleſſed
vvill , that by this meanes , yee may be founde not
only fauorers, but alſo follovvers, not only talkers,
but alſo vvalkers , not only louers , but alſo liuers,
not only proſeſſoures, but alſo practiſers, not only
vvorders , but alſo vvorkers of the holy ſctipture,
and ſo become bleſſed, as our Sauiour Chriſt ſaith.
Ifyee knovve theſe thinges, and doo them , bleſſed
are yee. For not euery one that ſaith vnto me Lord,
Lorde, shall enter into the kingdome of heauen,
but he that doth the vvill of the ſather, vvhich is in
heauen , he shal' enter into the kingdome of heauen. Yee are my ſreendes, yf you doo thoſe thinges
that I commaunde you . He that hath my commaundements , and keepeth them, he it is that loueth me. For in the ſight of god, as The apoſtle ſaith
they are not righteous, vvhich heare the lavve, but
the doers of the lavve shall be iuſtified. If any man
                        be

Iude.Epiſt.

Matth. 25.

Romans, 2.

be in Chriſt, he is a newe creature. They truly that
are Chriſtes, haue crucified the fleſh, with the affections and luſtes. VVe are the workmanſhip of
God, created in Chriſt Ieſu vnto good workes,
which God hath ordayned, that we ſhould walke
in them. Let our eares learne ſaith Saint Paul, to
excell in good workes, as farre foorth as neede requireth, that they be not vnfruitefull. Herein is my
father glorified (ſaieth our Sauiour Chriſt) that ye
beare much fruite, and become my Diſciples. Ye
haue not choſen me, but I haue choſen you, and
ordayned you to goe and bring foorth fruite, and
that your fruite ſhould remaine.

Goe therefore foorth (right worſhipfull and
dearely beloued) as ye haue begun, in the way of
righteouſneſſe. Receaue the Goſpell of Chriſte,
which is the worde of your ſaluacion, and bread
of life, with greedy, and deſirous mindes. Call on
God dayly (as ye doo) with feruent prayer, and
ceaſe not to be thankfull vnto him, for his benefits.
Be an example in life and conuerſacion, to them
that are vnder you. Seke the quietneſſe, and com-
modity of your Towne, and of the inhabitauntes
of the ſame, rather then your owne gaine, and
profite: ſtudy rather to be loued, then feared. To
the wicked and ſinfull, be ſeuere and ſharpe: but
to the good and godly, be gentle and louing. Continue your goodneſſes and liberalitie to the poore
ſtrangers which are exiled for the teſtimony of the
Lorde Ieſus, and tender them, as your ſelues. Suffer
not idleneſſe to creepe within the bounds of your
towne, but rather prouide that al be well & vertu-
ouſly occupied. Of the poore, haue diligent conſi-
deration.

Galat. .5.
Ephe. .2.

Tit. .3.

Ioan. .15.

deratiõ, but as for the sturdy & lasie lubbers, vvhich gladly lyue of the labour of other mens handes, and hate to be vvell occupied them selues: eyther compell to vvoorke, or els banishe them your tovvne. Looke diligently to the bringing vp of your youth, eyther in good letters, or els in some vertuous exercices, that in time to come, they be not vnprofitable members of the common vveale. But aboue all thinges, see that they be brought vp in the nurture and feare of the Lorde, and in the knovvledge of his holy vvoord, that they may learne euen from their Cradles to serue their Lorde G O D in holynesse and righteousnesse all the dayes of the Lorde. And that this thing may the more conueniently be brought to passe, as ye haue earnestly entended, and to that end haue prouided large summes of money among your selues: so vvith al expedition prouide, that your Schoole may be erected and set vp, for the godly and vertuous education of your youth. So shall yon both doo a noble sacrifyce vnto God, deserue vvell of many, and also leaue to your posteritie a vvoorthy monument of a most vvoorthy enterprise. And to helpe sorvvarde some poynt of godly doctrine to be taught in your nevve erected Schoole. After I had finished this little treatise, entituled, The Demaundes of holy Scripture, I thought it not vnsitting, not vnvvorthy our frēdship, to dedicate the same to your vvoorships, and so by you, to commend it to the Christian youth of your Schoole. In it they shall learne to knovve and vnderstand, the principall and cheefe povntes of Gods doctrine: so that by this meanes they shal be able to render a reason both of theyr fayth, and

doctrine,

doctrine, vvhich ~~they professe~~, and not be like Horses & Mules that ~~haue~~ no vnderstanding. The book is little, yf the number of the leaues be considered: but yf the matter therof be diligently pondered, it shalbe found both great, & profitable. Thus for this present, taking my leaue of you, I vvysh to you, and to the vvhole Tovvne, all good and prosperous things, both for yonr bodyes & soules, most humbly beseeching God, to finishe that good vvoorke; vvhich he hath begun in you, vnto the glory of his name, & vnto the profite of his holy congregation. Amen.

(·)

From my house at Caunterbury, the fyrst of September. 1563.

The Demaundes of

WHO did create *vs*⸗ God, who also made al *y* world of nought.

What things damned vs ? Sinne. In so much as Adam did eate, by the perswasion of Eua, of the Apple forbidden him of God . For sinne, is the breaking of the commaunde-mentes of GOD.

Who redemed vs, and set vs in the fauour of GOD againe ? Jesus Christ, by takyng our nature on him.

What is God vnto vs ? Wheras before he was a seuere & straight Iudge: through Christe he is become our most louing tender, and mercifull father.

What are we ? His dearely beloued chil-dren.

What thing is GOD ? An infinite sub-staunce , which onely with his word of might , did create and make all thinges, and with his most high and incompara-ble wisdome gouerneth all thing , and of his inestimable goodnesse, suffereth and preserueth all thing . I call that infinite

doth

B i.

Gene. 1.
Eccle. 18.
psalme. 14.
Acte. 14.17.
Romans. 5.
Gene. 3.
What sin is.

Gene. 3.
Romans. 5
1.Timoth.2
Romans. 5.
Ephe. 1. 2
Colossi. 1
1. Ioan. 3.
Ioan. 1
Galath. 4

What God is.

God is infi-nite.

both which hath neyther beginning no2 ending, and that which can not be comprehended, no2 compassed by mans b2aine, what thing it is. And in both these significacions God is infinite. Furthermo2e that is to euery man god o2 a god, that he loueth, d2eadeth, and wo2shippeth with all his hart. The Scripture also calleth the Judges and Officers of the earth gods.

Exodus. 22.
Pfalme. 82.

What a strange God is.

What is a strange God, or an other God? What soeuer thing we wo2shyp besides the very lyuing God. And that also that doth alienate and turneth our harte from Gods wo2de, is called a strang o2 an other God.

What faith is.

Romans. 10.
Hebru. 11.

What thing is fayth? It is a full and perfite confidence and trust in God th2ough Ch2iste, ingend2ed in our harte, by hearing the wo2de of God, and as Paul defineth faith: Faith is a sure confidence, of thinges which we looke fo2, and the certaintie ot p2omises.

What hope is.

What is hope? A styffe and firme expectacion, of such thinges as be p2omised vs of the wo2de of GOD.

What charitie is,

What is charitie? The p2incipall fruit of faith, a p2omple and redy wyll to do

good

good to our neighbour. Otherwhyles the Math 25. workes of mercie are called charitie.

What is the lawe? It is the liuely wyll *What the* of God, geuen vs by commaundement, as *law of god* well in the newe testament as in the olde, *is .* whose worke and operacion is to shewe *The office* sinne, to shewe that God is angry with vs *of the law.* for our euill doing, and dayly transgression Ioan. 7. of his commaundement, whose duty is to Romans. 7. accuse vs in our conscience, to cast vs 2. Cor. 3. downe, and make vs seeme vyle & nought Galat. 3. worth in our sight, and by this meanes, eyther bringeth vs to vtter desperacion, or els leadeth vs (as it were by the hande) to Christe, the only true pacifier of the conscience.

What is the Gospel? It is a glad tiding. *What the* Or els you may call it euery promise that *Gospell is .* God made of Christe, and of other his good benefites, wyerby the cloudes of the conscience be put awaye, and mans minde erected and made mery, whether these promises be in ye new testament, or in the old: Paule, saith it is the power of God, where Romans. 1. by all that beleeue are brought to healthe and sauegarde.

What is it to be a godly man, or who is
B ii. *godly?*

Who is godly.

godly? He oz shee that hath faith, and the feare of God befoze their eyes.

Who is vngodly.

Who is wicked, or vngodly? He oz shee that beleeueth not the pzomise of God, and that hath not the dzeade of God befoze them.

Who is a Christian.

Who is a Christian man? He that beleeueth on Chziste, and liueth accozding to his wozde.

Who is an Ethnike.

Who is an Ethnike or Miscreant? He that vseth not those lawes, and ozdinaunces, and hath not the faith that we haue, Oz els he that seeketh to be saued by some other meanes then by Chzist.

An Heretike, who.

Who is an Heretik? He which thinketh, and styfly mainteineth any thing against the doctrine of faith (that is to say)

The word of God is the doctrin of faith.

the wozd of God. Marke here the wozd of God, to be called the doctrine of faith, because faith, dzaweth from no whence els her pzinciples: then from the wozde of God. Because she only learneth, marketh, and beareth away the wozd of God.

The kingdom of Heauen what it is.

What is the kingdome of Heauen? It is where the wozd of God is truly pzeached and receiued, and where it beareth fruite meete foz the doctrine, whose king and

and Lo2d, is Chzift.

What is the worlde? An heape and
muftre of men, without the wo2d of God,
among whom the wo2d of God is despised
and persecuted: where is a rablement of al
vices, whose Pzince and God is Sathan.
In some place it is called an hot voyling
Sea, which can not reft and be affwaged.

The world what it is.

What is the word of God? It is the decreed sentence, wo2d, and will of God, ex-
p2effed and left behind of the Pzophetes
and Apoftles to vs, in ÿ canonical bookes
of the newe teftament and the old, whiche
wo2d he that reciueth (that is to say know-
ledgeth in his hart to be true and holy, and
liueth acco2ding to it) receiueth God, and
he that refufeth it, despiseth God, and as
much as lieth in him, he maketh God a
lyer. The wo2d of God hath sund2y names
in Scripture: as the swo2d of the spirite, a
two edged swo2d, a fire swo2d, an iron wal,
a ftrong hold, a well fenfed towne, confu-
ming fire. It is also called whete, the rod
of the mouth of the Lo2d, the b2eth of the
niouth of the Lo2de, a myfterie, an o2acle,
the p2int o2 fecreat wyll of the Lo2d.

The word of God what it is.

The nams of the worde of God.
Ephe. 6.
Heb. 4.
Iere. 22.
2. Theff. 2.

What are mans tradicions? What fo-
euer

B iii.

What mens tra-

ditions
are.

Math. 13
Iere. 23.
Math. 15.
Marke. 7.
Math. 19

euer mans reason hath, oz doth imagen
without the word of God, and ordeyneth
and wylleth it to be reputed and taken as
good, godly, and pleasant in the sight of
God. They be called in Scripture Cocle,
and Chaffe. Of these speaketh Christe,
where he saith. They do serue me in vaine,
whyle they teach such doctrine as are nothing but the commaundementes of men.

How men
are good

Who be good? Only God is good.
Notwithstanding, because all they that
haue the spirite of God, and are ruled by
his word, be of the flocke of God, and vnder his keeping: therefore God doth communicate and imparte his goodnesse to
them, and so they be called good, as theyr
Father, Lord, and Gouernour is.

Who be
euill.

Who be euill? They that haue not ý spirite of God, noz be ruled by his word, whether they liue vpright outwardly, and according of the letter of the lawe: as *Cato,
Socrates*, and they that be counted good
and vertuous among the Turkes, and
Iewes, oz els they that be open transgres-
sours of the lawe. For in Christ only is
saluacion and remission of sinnes. And vnto that time that our sinnes be remitted,
we

Acte. 4.
Ephe. 2.

we be euill, vncleane, and vnder dampna-
cion. And on this fashion we are all euyll,
and sinners by nature.

Who is iust or righteous? He that hath
faith. For through faith we are iustified.
To be iustified is to haue our sinnes not
imputed vnto vs, but to haue them forgeuen in Christ, and for Christ. Euen as Dauid saith: blessed are they whose vnrighte-
ousnesses are forgeuen, and whose sinnes
are couered. Blessed is that man to whom
the Lord imputeth no sinne. Now because
the faithful man only receiueth and enioyeth this mercie forgeuenesse, and this no
imputing of sinne through faith, therefore
he is called iust, and we through faith said
to be iustified. Sometime in Scripture
the Hipocrites, and they that thinke to be
saued by their workes, are called iuste or
righteous as we rede. I came not for the
righteous, &c.

Who is vnrighteous? He that hath no
faith.

What is euerlasting life? It is the tast
of the fauour and manifold mercies of
God, the peace of the conscience, a feruent
desire of Heauen, and to be with Christ.

B iiii.

*Who is
righteous.*
*What it
is to be
iustified.*
Psalm. 32.
Rom. 4.

Rom. 4. 5.
Gal. 2. 3.

*Vnrighte-
ous who.*
*Euerlas-
ting life
what.*

which

which the holy Ghost doth kendle in the hartes of the faithfull. Otherwhiles euerlasting life is called to knowe the very liuing God, & Iesus Christ, who ..z he sent downe. As it is sayd: He that hath the Sonne and beleeueth in him: hath euerlasting life.

Ioan. 17.
Ioan. 5.

What is euerlasting death, or hell? In this life it is the perpetuall grudge and horrible feare of conscience, the distresse and tediousnesse of the minde, dreding the wrath of God, which the deuil increaseth in the vnfaithfull: as it is plainely declared. Also hell is taken for extreme temptacion, which almost leadeth vs downe to desperacion: as we rede: The Lord leadeth vs downe to hell, and bringeth vs vp againe.

Hell, or euerlasting death, what it is

After this life it betokeneth the fire of Hell, where the damned soules be. It is called also a fyrie furnesse, and the vtter darknesse, where is wayling and gnashing of teeth, and vtter desperacion of the mercy of God.

Hell diuersly taken.
1. Reg. 2.
Esay. 66.
Apoc. 22.
Math. 13.
22. 25.

What thing is the blessing of God? It is the fauour, the grace, the helpe and beneficence of God. &c.

What the blessing of God is.

What

What is the curſe of God? It is the an- *What the curſe of God is.*
gre, extreme wrath, and the lacke of al the
good benefites of God.

What is a good conſcience? It is the *What a good conſcience is.*
peace of the mind, a ſpirituall ioy, and a
plaine feeling and perceiuing of the goodneſſe of God towardes vs, through fayth
in Ieſus Chriſt, which is deſcribed and ſet
out. And is no more to ſay, but that when
we perceiue that through faith in Ieſus Rom. 5.
Eſay. 57. 35
Chriſt, our ſinnes be forgeuen, and that we
be in the fauour of God: we be harte hole,
mery, and ſound.

What is an euill conſcience? It is an *What an euyl con-ſcience is.*
inward boyling heate, and toſſing of the
minde, for a mans wickedneſſe, and when
for pure anguiſh of the ſight and horrore
of ſinne, the hart fainteth and failleth him.
It is called in Scripture the worme of the
conſcience.

What is veritie, and truth? Chriſt him
ſelfe, the word of God, and what ſoeuer
els agreeth with the word of God. For as
Chriſt ſaith I am the way, the truth, and
the life. Also, thy wordes be the truth.
There is also a Ciuile truth, or veritie (as
it is called) and that is when with that
　　　　　　B v.　　　which

Ioan. 14.
Ioan. 17.
which is sayd, the thing agreeth, & when we find words agreeing with the thing it selfe.

What fal-shod is.
What is lesing, or falsitie? What soeuer thing is euemie, and not agreeing to the truth and the word of God: as mans tradicions, or doctrines that serue not to the same word of God.

The feare of God what it is.
What is the feare of God? Suche an humblenes and lowe behauiour as natu-rall sonnes haue towardes their louing fa-thers. It is also a redy, glad, and wylfull warenesse in ordering our selues, that we do not commit any thing against God, and his word, for feare least we should of-fend so louing and tender a father. Which feare, as it spzingeth only out of faith, so it is only in y faithful. Then we feare God wisely: when with hart and mind, we so endeuer to liue and order our selues: as yf we had God a witnesse and looker of all our deedes, wordes, ye and of our preuis thoughtes and cogitacions. This louing preade ingendereth wisedome and bzing-eth Gods blessing on vs, and dziueth out sinne out of the bzest. The seruile and bond feare is the amasing, dzede, and abasshing
of

of the mind, that the wicked men haue of the wrath of God, ingendred by laying the lawe to their euill liuing. Rom. 8.

What is the contempt of God? A despising, or a light regarding of the doctrine and the commaundementes of God, proceeding of an vncleane hart and wicked minde, a pleasure and delight in sinne and ignoraunce, the roote of all mischiefe, which fruite of incredulitie, God neuer left vnpunished, as it appeereth. Exo. and Nume. &c.

What the contempt or despysing of God is.

What is thankes geuing? It is a remembraunce, and a thankful acknowledging of the benefites of God: when we surely thinke all that we haue commeth of him. It is called in the Scripture, sacrifice of prayse geuing.

Thankes geuing what it is: Psalm. 50.

What is vnkindnesse, and priuie murmuring against God? It is to grudge, and not to be content with the workes of God, and to forget his benefites. Examples hereof we rede.

Vnkindnesse and murmuring against God what it is. Exod. 16. 17.

What is it to haue the holy Ghost? To be godly disposed, and to haue an heauenly burning in the mind, euer vpright, whole, sincere, and pure, vertuous, alway iudging

To haue the holy Ghoste what it is.

iudging the best, willing and wishing wel to euery body, the fruites of whome be all vertues, which ye may see in the Gala-thians.

Galat. 5.

To be euill minded, or to haue the deuil what it is.

What is an euill mind, or to haue the de-uill? It is to haue an euil cancard mind, to be against God and his word, to be ge-uen all to wickednesse, to misdeeme and iudge all to the worst.

A good Angell, what it is.

What is a good Angell? The messen-ger of God, or what soeuer ye wyll, by which God worketh vs, and in vs that that is good, profitable, and commodious.

An euill Angell, what it is.

What is Sathan, or an euill Angel? An aduersary and enemy of God, a worker of al mischefe & death vnto vs. Otherwhiles it is put only for the deuill.

The Crosse what it is

What is the Crosse? It is all manner of greuaunce geuen to euery manner of vocation & kind of life, grounded on faith and the word of God, & what that we doo, goeth not forward as we would. It is also the teaching, warning, chastising rod, and staffe of the Lord, which names be for to be seene in the prouerbes and psalmes.

What the Crosse of Christe is.

The Crosse of Christ, is his passion and the preaching of the same, and the persecution

tion that followeth the preachers and beleeuers of the same.

What is pleasure, and the ease of this life? It is when we haue all at will, when God leaueth vs to our selues, and troubleth vs not with any aduersitie for faith and the word of God. *What the pleasure and ease of this life is.*

What is sinne? It is the transgression, and breaking of any of Gods commaundementes. It is also a naturall propencion and inclinacion to noughtinesse, ingendred with vs at our byrth. What soeuer is not of faith, is sinne. It is also the distrust in God, and the ignoraunce and contempt of him, and a trust and confidence in our owne workes. *What sinne is.*

What is originall sinne? It is the poyson and corruption that we haue in our birth, through the infection of our nature in Adam, which doth bring foorth in vs the fruite of incredulitie, and all wickednesse, and maketh vs vnable to the workes of the lawe, as the lawe requireth them to be done of vs: vntill Christ and his word hath made vs a newe creature. *Originall sinne what it is.*

What is originall Iustice? The integritie, holenesse, & soundnesse of the powers *Originall iustice what it is.*

ers of the body and the soule, whereby both the soule and the body could verely obey, doo, and fulfill the lawe of God. Wherefore after the poison of sin entred: nature lost her integritie and soundnesse, and the venim of sinne made weake, faint, and feeble the whole nature of man, so that it could not in no wise wil or do the worke, that it whole before could do. And not this only, but it infected and corrupted the flesh and the soule, and all the powers of them both, which infection ingendred in the nature of man thus febled, the ignoraunce and contempt of God, the distrust in God, the murmuring against God when he sendeth aduersitie, or sicknesse. It causeth furthermore man to be without the feare of God, to hate the iudgement of God, to flee and runne away from God when he chasteneth vs, to be angry with him and dispayre, and to trust in thinges corruptible, &c. These be the horrible biles, sores, pockes, and carbucles that disfigure the face of man. Which though they be neuer so high, yet our schole men and canonistes (I meane the professours of the Byshop of Romes lawes) coule neuer see, or perceiue.

Rom. 7.
a. Cor. 3.

The corruption of the nature of man.

ceyue. These Chrifte through faith at our baptifme doth fuppreffe and abate theyr power, and at the laft by death doth vtterly vainquifhe and kill.

What meane you by thefe wordes, Pœna, *and* Culpa? This word Culpa, which is in englifh a faute, or trefpaffe properly, in this place betokeneth the gilt (as we call it) or the trefpaffe, and that which the law punifheth in the deede or fact: as in an act of felony, the law punifheth not the comming to the Horfe, nor yet the brydeling, no nor the leading of the Horfe from the ftable, medowe, or common, for all thefe may be doone without the euill and vnlawfull defire of the Horfe, and agayne with the owners leaue. But the lawe punifheth the comming, the brydeling, and taking away the Horfe againft the owners wyll, and with the mind of ftealing him, and calleth the facte chefte, or felony. This word, Pœna (which is in Englyfhe payne) is the wages and punifhment taken for the faute. And thus fome kinde of vices, al hurtes, damages, ficknesse, peftilences, perils, errours, and the lacke of Gods word that we haue among vs: be paines,

What this word Cul-pa figni-fieth.

What this word Pœna *fignifieth.*

paines, and punishmentes of sinne, That
God punisheth sinne with losse and daunger both of body & goodes, with sicknesse,
pestilence, and such other (none I thinke
doubteth) but that he punisheth sinne by
sinne, and sinne by errours and heresies:
the worlde can not so clerely perceiue.

Rom. 2.

Howe be it Paul, doth playnly declare it,
where he sayth : because the Gentils turned the glory of God, and worshiped the
creature more then the maker, &c. Therefore (saith he) God gaue them vp vnto
shameful lustes,&c. Which lustes be there
straight after expressed. And this punishment (I meane to punish sinne by sinne)
is a very sore punishment.

He punisheth sinne by errours and heresies thus. When the word of God is plen-
teously and sincerely preached (as it is
nowe) and yet men still kicke against it,
or in case many receiue it, yet fewe or non
regard it, or liue according to it, but with
their wordes make on it only for a fleshly
libertie:then(I say) God taketh his word
away from thence (as who be not worthy
of it) and letteth the worlde preuaile a-
gainst his preachers, and suffreth Ante-
christe

chriſte (who muſt nedes ſucceede Chriſt) to kill them, ſo that Antichriſte peaceably **Math. 5.** enioyeth his kingdome (as he hath doone all ready this great while) and he muſt needes haue like doctrine to him ſelfe. So did he puniſhe the Iewes his owne elec- **Note wel.** ted people at ſundry times more then .ii. M̃. yeere, and ſuffered them to worſhip falſe Gods, or els to ſet vp their owne tra- dicions, Gods preceptes neglected. So alſo hath he puniſhed our fore fathers theſe viii. or ix. C. peeres. And now except we thankefully receyue his woord, and liue thereafter in the newneſſe of life, ac- cording as we are called (no doubt of it) he wyll, not only reuolue and caſt vs downe againe to our old ignorounce, cap- tiuitie and bondage: but alſo ſhortly take ſuch vengeaunce on vs, as he threatened Bethſaida, Corazin, &c.

Nowe God remitteth the crime, gylte, and treſpace to his electe through faith in Chriſte: but he reſerueth (after a certayne manner) a little porcion of the paine (not to counterpeiſe therewith, or ſatiſfy his iuſtice for the crime, as the Byſhop of Rome with his complices hath taught vs

this

God puni-
sheth sinne
in this
worlde, not
after thys
life in pur-
gatory, as
the Papis-
tes faine.

this great while) but to chastise their flesh with all, and sometime to be an example vnto other to forbeare like crimes, for fear of like punishment, or to declare the yre of God for such crimes. So that what trouble, vexacion, griefe, losse, sicknesse so euer the best men that be, haue: they deserue it with much more. Howbeit (no not thus) GOD would beate, scourge, and trye his: and it were not for their owne profite and auayle. For by this meanes he nourtereth, reineth, and humbleth his electe, that they may knowe them selues the better, and lest they runne at large after the world: as it appeareth by the aduoutry of

1. Cor. 11.
2. Reg. 12.

Dauid, and many other storyes in the Byble.

Innocencie
what it is.

What is innocencie? The purenesse of the minde, and when the conscience is not giltie, or findeth it selfe culpable in any thing. This innocency only the fayth in Iesus Christe ingendereth in vs. In this state was Paule (after many interpreters mindes) when he sayd. I knowe nought by my selfe. &c. He sayd not this, that he thought not him selfe a sinner, and that he trespassed not afore God (for then had he

ben

ben a lyer. For Moyses saith to the Lord:
it is thou that takest away trespasse, ini-
quitie, and sinne, and none innocent before
thee) but he meaneth of his conuersacion.
In this state also was Ezechias the good
King, when he turned him to the wal, and
wepte. Here we call, not to be giltie, or culpable, to haue the peace of the conscience,
and ȳ is when we beleeue through Christe
that our sinnes be hid, for vnto that time,
the lawe ceaseth not to accuse vs in our
conscience.

What is the spirite? It is a Heauenly
sence, or vnderstanding, springing out of
the worde of God (or els the selfe word of
God) exceeding the sence of the fleshe and
reason. The wordes that I speake vnto
you, they be spirite and life: meaning they
amount and passe the fleshe and sence of
reason, they be spirituall and heauenly. It
is sometime put for what so euer liueth
and breatheth: as all the spirits prayse ye
the Lorde, sometime for the breath and
winde

What is the fleshe? Euery affection,
the hart, the minde, and thought of man,
and what so euer els man doth, or can do

C ii.   by

In margin:
1. Cor. 4.
1. Ioan. 1.
Exod. 34.

4. Reg. 20.

What the spirite is.

Ioan. 6.

Psalm. 150.
Ioan. 3.

What the fleshe is.

by al the powers of his reason, destitute of the worde of God. For Christe saith. That which is borne of the fleshe, that is, it vnderstandeth not thinges that be spirituall. Fleshe other while betokeneth the letter and fleshly vnderstanding. The fleshe profiteth nothing, it is the spirite that quickeneth.

Ioan. 3.
1. Cor. 2.
Ioan. 6.

What is the newe man? It is the man that is renued and borne againe by faith and the worde, through the spirite of God. Except a man be borne a new, he can not se the kingdome of heauen. To be borne a-newe he calleth, where as before we were but carnall and fleshly, not vnderstanding the misteryes of the spirite, we must be borne agayne in spirite (that is) to become spirituall and more meete to vnderstande spirituall thinges.

What the newe man is.
Ioan. 3.

What is the olde man? Our affections, appetites, and vnderstanding according to reason, without faith : euen as we be all naturally borne of our mother, as it appeareth in diuers places of the Scripture. Also the whole body of sinne is called the old man in Scripture, and they liue according to the old man, that liue in ignoraunce,

What the old man is.
Psalm. 51.

raunce, and followe the luskes of their Ephe. 2.
hart, not walking in the newnesse of lyfe. Coloss. 2.

Who is blessed, or happy? All be it I Blessed, or may aunswere with Christ: blessed is he, *happy* that heareth and kepeth the woorde of *who.* God: yet is he otherwyse defined in the Luke. 12. Scripture. As he is to be thought happy, who holdeth him selfe well content with his fortune, and thankefully recep= ueth whatsoeuer God sendeth him, and who is at one with God and al creatures, that is, doth not murmure against God, and on the other side enuieth nor dispiseth any man.

Who is a wretch, or vnhappy? He that *Who is* holdeth not him selfe content with that *vnhappy.* that God hath sent him. He with whome nothing goeth forwarde, nor agreeth not with God nor man.

Who is poore? He that can not make *Poore* any great boastes, or crakes of himselfe, *who is.* and who is destitute of all helpe, as be they, of whome Christe saith: blessed are the poore in spirite, in Scripture he is called lowe, humble, and hungry, and he Math. 5. who is nowe in aduersitie.

Who is riche? He is called riche in Ritch
    C iii.   Scripture, *who is.*
                        Luke. 1. 6.

Scripture, which needeth no helpe concerning his saluacion, but hath workes ynough, and more then ynoughe to bring him to heauen. And (as a man may call it) full vp to the throte of the righteousnesse: as be all Hipocrites, Phariseies, and iustifiers of them selues, they also be called riche in Scripture, which be proud, mighty, and dronken with fortune and prosperitie, euer polling the poore.

Wise and circum-spect who.

Who is wyse, and circumspect? He which knoweth God and his worde, which (when he doubteth) asketh counsell, and doth all thing thereafter.

A foole who.

Who is a foole? He that rashly is caried hither and thither, with euery mocion, that considereth nothing, regardeth nothing, nor suffereth himselfe to be corrected, and warned of his euill doing, but headlong runneth as he began: forsing not whether he sinke, or swymme, or what becommeth of him, and who as he knoweth not the worde of God, so he passeth not on it. The wisedome of God taken as foolishnesse before the worlde, is the preaching of the Crosse of Christ, and the iustifiing by faith (that is to say) though to suffer

persecution

Luke. 16.
Iac. 5.

persecution for the worde of God, and to preach that we iustified by faith, be godly and the wisedome of the spirite : yet the world laugheth it to scorne, and counteth it highe foolishenesse. The wisedome of the fleshe, is foolishnesse before God.

1. Cor. 3.

What is a childe, or to be a childe? A childe in Scripture, is a wicked man, or he that is ignorant, and not exercised in godlynesse and Gods word be he olde, or be he young. Or he that lacketh spirituall iudgemēt in discerning & chosing things. Wo be to the comtrey whose King is a childe. And he shall die a childe of a .C. yeere olde, A child also is sometime taken for humble or meke. Who soeuer hūbleth him selfe as this childe, is greatest in the kingdome of Heauen.

A child what.

Eccl. 10.
Esay. 65.
Math. 18.

What is an olde man, auncient, or elder? He which is well taught and instructed in the worde of God, and exercised therein. He which liueth honestly, and without reprofe hauing horenesse of maners, authoritie, grauitie, and high knowledge in the worde of God.

What an Elder is.

What is Christe? The annointed king and priest of God, sitting on ý right hande

What Christe is.

Exod. 19.
1. Pet. 2.
Apoc. 1.
of the father, hauing full power to defend and warrant his flocke, and being a ready aduocate for his at their neede. And by him all Christen men be annoynted kings and priestes. They be called kinges, when in Christe, and through Christe they subdue their wylde affections, the diuell, and death. They be called priestes, and sacrificers, when they offer vp their bodyes into a liuely, holy, and acceptable sacrifice

Romans.12.
vnto God, which is our reasonable seruing of God.

What Antichrist is.
What is Antichriste? The aduersary of Christe, and he which goeth about to obscure, or vtterly to abrogate and pull away his glory: teaching, defining, and determining, that Christe is not the king, priest, and aduocate of his flocke.

Prayer what is is.
What is prayer? A brenning desire, or peticion of the minde, lift vp and directed vnto God (springing and comming of the neede and lacke that we find in our selfe) as farre forth as faith and the promise of God suffereth and permitteth vs, where marke that we aske such thinges as be honest and lawfull. Sometime it is taken for the lifting vp of the handes, the desire, crying

crying and sighing of the poore, and such as stand in neede. And some doth call it more generally the lifting vp of the mind to God.

What is temptation? The profe and trial of our faith, and an exercise and practise of the worde. Otherwhiles it is called the rod and staffe of the Lorde, and the discipline whereby we see our selues, and perceyue how well we haue profited and gon forwarde in the word which may best be tryed, then when that we goe about doth not goe forward as we woulde. *Tempta-cion what it is.*

What is desperacion? It is when in temptacion, and such trying of vs (wheither it be by aduersitie, or any other thing) we fall downe distrust, and cast away all hope of the mercie and goodnesse of God: then (I say) when of no side appeareth any hope, or succor, and when we be, as seemeth to vs) vtterly forgotten and cast away of God. Of which temptacion we may see a manifest example. To speake properly desperacion is the vtter and finall dispayre and distrust of helpe. *Despera-tion what is is.*

Iob. 7.

VVhat is vocacion, or calling? It is the manner of life, vnto which God hath cal- *Vocation, or calling what it is.*

C v.   led

led thee . Or els the common consent (as Mayres and other Officers) or els thou hast appoynted and purposed thy selfe vnto, by thy owne accorde. Or els ye may call it euery kinde of life, in which we exercise faith and charity. To be called to the kingdome of heauē, is to heare ý worde of god. To be chose or elected, is to beleue it.

Math. 20.

Predesti-
nation
what it is.

Rom. 9. 10.
11.

VVhat is predestinacion? It is the secrete election of the wysedome of God to eternall life, without our deseruing. They be predestinate and called to euerlasting life which heare & receiue the word of god.

Free wyll
what it is.

VVhat is free wyll? It is the libertie that man hath in doing outward thinges, and the naturall worke of man in suche thinges as be not spirituall: as in ordering him selfe after a ciuill and politicall fashion, and outwarde fulfilling of the moral vertues. Howbeit, he hath not the power, nor nor yet the wil to loue God, dreade God, and to know him: vntill that he be renued, and that Christ hath set him at libertie. For then (as Iohn saith) If the sonne hath made ye free, then are ye free in deede. For vnto that time that we know

Ioan. 8.

God, we can not loue him nor dreade him.

And

And when we loue him, and dreade him, then haue we power through him, to kepe the lawe. Yet when man was in the state of originall iustice, that is to say, when he had the integritie, wholenesse & soundnesse of the powers of the body and soule, then might he obey, doo, and fulfill freely the lawe of God, but after the poyson of sinne entred, it made weake and feble the whole nature of man.

VVhat is the temple of God? A pure, cleane, and single hart, without all gyle, fraude, and doublenesse. Also the Church, wherein God is worshipped.

VVhat is the Church, or congregation of Christe? It is the company, assemblement, and consent of good men on the worde of God, and in the faith of Iesus Christe.

VVhat is the Church of Sathan? It is the multitude of wicked men conspiring against God and his word.

VVhat is the Sabboth day, or to keepe holy day? It is to abstayne from the outward workes of the flesshe, and to pray vnto God in spirite, heare his word, and to haue our minde set on his lawe, after what manner

Eccl. 15.

The temple of God what it is.
1. Cor. 3.
2. Cor. 6.
The church what it is.
The church of Christe.
The Church of Sathan.
To keepe holy day what it is.
Esay. 56.

manner true Chriſtians euer keepe the lawe. You may els ſay, that the holy day is wherein we remember the benefites of God, and geue him thankes for them.

Grace, what it is.
VVhat is grace? The good wil of God towarde vs, his fauour and bounteous goodneſſe, freely employed on vs without our deſeruing.

Merites & workes what.
VVhat be merites and workes? They be called and counted in Scripture to be the refuſing and contempt of the fauoure of God, and a confidence to be ſaued by a mans owne power, ſtrength, & deſertes.

The name of God what it is.
VVhat is the name of God? It is what ſoeuer pertaineth to God, or els to euery name which we aſſigne vnto God & cal him by: as the God of hoſtes, the ſtrong and gelous God. &c. Alſo his glory honor and maieſty.

What it is to ſhew the word of God.
To ſhewe the word of God, is to preache ſincerely the Goſpell, that is to ſay, that all that beleeue haue theyr ſinnes forgeuen them, that they be deliuered from death and hell, and hath geuen them euerlaſting life freely through Ieſus Chriſte.

To ſerue God what it is.
VVhat is it to ſerue God? To liue according to his word, to beleeue and put

truſt

trust in him, to referre all thinges vnto his glory, and to loue and helpe our neighbour.

VVhat is it to serue the deuill? It is to resist the word, to serue Mammon, his belly, his fleshly appetites, the world, and carnall affections. *To serue the deuill what it is.*

VVhat is to worship God? It is not only to pray vnto him, but also to shewe and exhibyte in the outward gesture honour and reuerence vnto him. *To worship God what it is.*

VVhat is to beleeue in God? It is wholy to commit a mans owne selfe in all matters to him, and to haue a sure hope in him selfe, that what soeuer God promiseth shall be perfourmed. *To beleeue in God what it is.*

VVhat is to fast? To beware lest we ouer lade our body with surfetting, in meates or drinkes, that we liue chastly and soberly, to abstayne from vyce, to kepe our body lowe, geuing it that only that is necessary. *To fast what is is.* Luke, 21.

VVhat is it to folow Christe? It is to beleeue in him, to marke and followe his doctrine, and to followe him whether soeuer he leadeth vs, or calleth vs, and to suffer wyllingly what soeuer he layeth on *To folowe Christ what it is.*

our

our backes.

What it is to leaue all things for Christes sake. VVhat is to leaue and forsake all that a man hath, to sell all, and to denye a mans selfe? To leaue, forsake, and sell, is to repute & recken such thinges as we haue, as none of ours, yea, gladly to forsake and leaue for Christes sake (if the matter came to that poynt) wyfe, chyldren, parentes, countrey, house, land, and all other suche, in so much that (yf neede required) we woulde (for Christes sake and the Gospels quarell) offer our selfe to all dangers, and death at conclusion.

To deny a mans selfe what it is. To deny a mans selfe, is frankely and freely to graunt his workes, and all his other good indeuerringes to be vnable to his saluacion, and vtterly to kill the old Adam in him with all his affections.

To visite what it is. What is it to visite? When it is taken in the good part, it betokeneth that God looketh vpon, and sendeth his benefites some whether. The Lord hath visited his

Luke. 7. people. When it is taken in the euil part, it betokeneth as much as the Lorde punisheth and scourgeth wicked and cursed, when he taketh vengeaunce on them for

Exo. 20. their wickednesse: as I the Lord thy God

am

am a iealous God, visiting the sinnes of the fathers vpon the children, vnto ẙ third & fourth generatiõ of them ẙ hate me,&c.

What is the hand of God? It is the power, or strength of the Lord, whereby he helpeth and doth good vnto the godly, and whereby he worketh mischiefe and taketh vengeaunce on the cursed. *What the hand of God is.*

The arme of God betokeneth the power of him, and Christe him selfe, whereof ye may read abundantly. *The arme of God. Esay. 54.*

The finger betokeneth the holy Ghoste. *The finger of GOD.*

What be the eyes of God? The respect, care, and regarde that he hath vpon the good, and his gentilnesse, mercy and redinesse to defend them. *Luke. 13. The eyes of God.*

His countenaunce is taken for ẙ straight and narowe looking of the wicked to their destruction and perdition. The eyes of the Lord be on the righteous, and his eares attend vnto their prayers. But the countenaunce of the Lord is vpon the sinners. His face betokeneth fauour, beneuolence, and the gladnesse in the Lord. But as sone as thou hast turned thy face, they shall be confused, and wyll turne againe vnto their earth. The mouth of the Lord hath great *The countenance of God. Psalm. 33. The face of GOD. Psalm. 103.*

vehemency

The mouth of the Lorde. Esay. 1

vehemency and pythe in it, for the Pro=
phetes when they will haue theyr wordes
marked and regarded say: the mouth of the
Lorde hath spoken this.

The outwarde appereaunce of any
thing is also called the face : as we say.
Iudge not according to the face and out=
warde sight.

What the face of the anger of God is. Abac. 2. Psalm. 67.

The face of y^e anger of God, is y^e feling of
the curse & wrath of God, also y^e presence,
sight, & iudgment of God is caled his face
as . Let al y^e earth hushe or be stil before
the face of the Lord . As the Waxe vadeth
and consumeth in the face of ye fire: so shal
all sinners perishe before the face of God.

The eye of man, what A single eye. A wycked eye. Math. 21. Math. 5.18.

What is the eye of man ? It is reason,
or the wysedome of the flesh. A single eye,
is reason instructed with ye word of God.

A wicked eye, is reason depraued and
corrupt, & enuye engendred against their
neighboure for the gyftes of God.

Otherwhiles the eye, hand, right foote, &c.
betoken our kinsmen and best belooued
freendes.

Feete what they signify. Psalm. 25.

What betoken feete in Scripture ? The
feete be and betoken the affections, desire,
and will of the harte . My foote stode
straight

straight foorth, that is to say, I haue ney- Psalm. 25.
ther hurt any man, nor would hurt. And To wash
though perchaunce I haue hurt any: yet I one an o-
willed none euill, or hated any.&c. To thers feete
washe one an others feete, is one to loue what it is.
an other, and to wyll well one to an other.

What is a slaunder, to offende, or to be of- Slaunder,
fendicle to any man? It is whereby the or offendi-
faith or charitie of our brother is offended cle what
or hurt. The faith of the brother is offen- it is.
ded when any man preacheth & teacheth
other thinges then the word of God.
Of this kind of slaunder speaketh Christ. Math. 18.
Who soeuer offendeth one of these little
ones.&c.

The charitie of our neighbour is offended or hurt, when we helpe not the poore,
when we be not glad of our neyghboures
prosperitie, and sory in his aduersitie.&c.

It is the obstacle and let, whereby we
fall and stomble in the way of the Lorde,
that is to say, we haue not a life vpright
and worthy the Lorde, I meane when we
stagger in the faith or loue towardes our
neighbour, in which two euery christian
ought stoutly and still to walke. Forget-
ting with saint Paule the thinges that be Phil. 3.

behind

behind our backes, endeuering to come to the marke set before our eyes.

Math.13.14. 15.

Otherwhiles slaunder, or offending is taken in Scripture for the offending wherby the wicked can not beare the word.

Hipocrite.
Enuious
man.

What is an Hipocrite? It is the wicked man coloured and cloked with godlynesse. Wherefore hipocrisy is called fayned holynesse.

Gen. 4.
1. Reg. 18.
2. Reg. 20.
Ioan. 3.
1. Reg. 18.

What is an enuious man? He whose hart for anger burneth at an other mans prosperitie, nor can suffer (with his will) any other to be enriched with the benefites of God . So did Cayn enuy Abell his brother, Saul Dauid, and Ioab Amasas. But Iohn did not enuy Christ his successour, when he sayd. He must increase, and I decrease . Nor Ionathas Saules sonne did not thus hate Dauid his loyall and trusty freende and companion.

God to
sleepe
what it is.

What is for God to sleepe? When he seemeth to vs to forsake vs in our temptation, nor helpeth vs. So slept Christe in the ship, his Apostles being in daunger and ieoperdye . And so doth Dauid call vpon God to awake: saying arise & wake Lorde, why doest thou sleepe so long?

Math. 8.

Psalm. 44

What

What is it for men to sleepe? When they without all care of the word of God, slugge and sleepe in sinne and ignoraunce, when they refuse, contemne, and regarde it not.

To rest and sleepe in the Lord: is to dye in fayth. &c.

What is to be awake? To exercise and put in vre the word of God, and our faith.

What is fortune? It is fate, or destiny chaunsing to any man by the will of God, without mans prouidence.

Who is my brother? He that hath one father with me, that is to say, God.

Who is my weake brother? He that hath one faith with me in God, and fauoureth the Gospell : but yet wauereth and doubteth in his conscience of some things: as meates and difference of dayes.

Who is my neighbour? He on whom I exercise charitie and loue, or hee who needeth my helpe.

Who is a Lorde or maister? He that hath a seruant, gouerneth and ruleth another: as he whiche keepeth vnder vices and lewde appetites, is Lord and maister ouer them, so through faith in Iesus

Men to sleepe what it is.

Math. 13. Ioan. 7.

To be awake.

Fortune.

Brother.
Math. 23.

Weake brothe
Rom. 14.

Neighboure.

Lorde, or Maister.

D.ii.   Christ,

Chrilt, we be Lordes ouer the Deuill, Death and sinne. Also he that vseth the Sabboth or holy daye as he seeth neede: that is to saye, doubteth not (if he see the loue of his neighbour requireth the contrarie) to breake it, that man I say, is the Lorde of the Sabboth day.

Mark. 2.

Seruaunt.
Ioan. 8.

Who is a seruant? He that hath a maister, and is not his owne man: or else he that is at the becke and commaundement of another.

Thus Paule calleth himselfe the seruant of Chrilt, as he that doth and accomplisheth the will of sinne, he is a seruaunt to sinne.

A true and
faithfull
seruaunt.
Matth. 24.

What is a true and faithfull seruaunt? He that hath fayth; and doth his duetie with all diligence, accordyng to his vocation and calling.

A slouth-
full and
vnfaith
full ser-
uaunte.

What is a slothfull and vnfaithfull seruaunt? He which beleeueth not in God, negligently ordereth himselfe in his vocacion, and refuseth to beare his crosse.

Magis-
trate.
Roma. 13.

What is an officer or ruler? Euery lawfull power among men, ordeined of God to the defence and protection of that that is good, and to prohibite and to punishe that

that

that is euill, accozding to right and equity.

What is a tyraunt? An vnlawfull and *Tirant.*
vniust ruler, which administreth all things
as he list, and laieth great burdens & yokes
vpon y people, doing against all conscience
& equity. Such a one was Pharao to the *Exod. 1.*
childzen of Israell. Howbeit, suche be not *Note well.*
to be resisted of Chzistian men, but obeyed
in all thinges saue where they wil haue vs
doo that that God fozbiddeth vs, and haue
vs not to do that that god biddeth. And we
must tarye till God deliuer vs out of suche
tyzauntes handes: as the childzen of Israe-
el did.

What is matrimony, or wedlocke? The *Matry-*
lawfull coupling and resozt of man and *mony.*
woman, accozding to the ozdinance and *Gen. 3.*
commaundement of God.

What is adultery? The vnlawful com= *Adultery.*
pany of man and woman: as is the mari-
age with the mother, sister, aunt, bzothers
wyfe, and such other, wherein Moyses
treateth. To that perteyneth stupze, incest,
fozinicacyon, and like abhominacions,
touched in the fozesaid Chapiters.

What is properly mans worke, or that *Mans*
man can doo? What soeuer that reason *worke.*

and the nature of man can inuent and doo: as to rule his house well , to gouerne the common weale, buylde, and searche the nature of thinges, and dispute and reason vpon them.

Workes passing mans power.

What is that that is aboue mans power, otherwise called spirituall and heauenly? Whatsoeuer surmounteth reason , and that man can not attaine vnto, except God graunteth it and geueth power to obtaine it : as that our sinnes be forgiuen through faith , and that we be saued by Iesus that dyed on the crosse. That God is our defender and louing father, yea in aduersitie and trouble . That God is iust, yea whē he suffereth the good men to be persecuted and troubled, And on the otherside , letteth the euill men to enioy and haue all their pleasure and will here, and preuaile against the good men.

Fleshe and bloud, what it is.

What is fleshe and bloud? The circumlocution and very descripcion of man. For man of him selfe is nothing but fleshlye and carnall . Blessed art thou Simon the

Ioan. 3.
Math. 16.

sonne of Ionas, for fleshe and bloude hath not opened this vnto thee , but my father that is in heauen, sayth Christ.

What

What is care and thought? A playne *Care and* token of diffidence and distrust in God. It *thought,* is an vnfaithfull care & pensifenesse of the *what it is.* minde for meate, drinke, clothing, and suche other necessaries, which, in whome soeuer you doe see it : surely it can not bee denied, but that he is destitute of fayth in God, and that his minde is set ouermuch to worldly things. Therefore I saye vnto you, be not carefull for the life, &c. After all such things doe the heathen seeke, sayeth *Math. 6.* Christ.

The care and thought of faith is prohibited by Gods worde. For faith onelye looketh and leaneth to Gods worde and promises.

Nowe to take thoughte and care least God will not fulfill his worde and promises, is to mistrust and not beleeue God, and so much as lyeth in vs, to make God a lyer. Wherefore, as I saide before, all thought and care of matters pertaining to faith, is vtterly to be put away.

The care and sorowe in thinges belonging to charitie and loue in euery mans vocation, is commaunded by Gods word, as one to be sorie for anothers mischaunce

D.iiii.   and

and miserie.

Gladnesse of harte what it is.

What is the gladnesse of the heart? A token of confidence in God, when in aduersitie, trouble, or affliction, wee wayle not, frowne or fret within our selues, but reioyce, looke stoutly on it, and holde our selues well apayde, hauing this euer before our eyes : The sonne whom G O D loueth and recepueth, he vseth to chasten and beate.

Prouerb . 3.
Heb. 12.

Cōtrariwise, it is also a token of worldly welthinesse, and delight in pleasures of the fleshe, whom God threatneth : Wo be vnto you that laugh here, for ye shall wepe and wayle, sayth Christ.

Luke. 6.

Sinne against the father and the sonne.
1. Timo. 1.

What is to sinne against the Father, and the Sonne ? It is to resist and persecute the worde of God : but yet by ignoraunce, and of a good zeale : as Paule did before he was conuerted.

Sinne against the holy Ghost.

What is the sinne against the holy ghost ? It is when any resisteth the open, manifest and knowne truth, when any beleeue not the open and playne promises of God, and when any dispaireth finally in the mercie of God.

Zeale what it

What is ment by this word Zeale in Scripture?

ture? Zeale, is anger medled and mixte *signifieth.*
with loue: as when the louing father is angry with his childe for doing amisse : he
doth it not because he hateth his sonne,
but in doing so he signifieth his fatherly
loue towardes him, willing by that, that
shall do no more so, but endeuer to better.
For when the childe is thus chidden or
beaten, he taketh heede that he doth not so
againe, for feare of a more grieuous punishment. It betokeneth also the anger
that chaunseth betwixt them that loue har-
tely togeather. &c.

From hence commeth iealousy, whiche *Iealousy.*
springeth out of vehement loue. God is *Why God*
called in Scripture a iealous God, not *is called a*
that because any should thinke that any *iealouse*
such affections were in God? But that *God.*
we might learne that God dooth all the
things that are done, for nothing else, but
for their sake onely, whome he loueth so
tenderly, euen his elect. Not bicause he
looketh for anye vauntage by it, but that
they may be saued, and enioye the kingdome prepared for them.

What is the bodie of Christ? The con- *The body*
gregation of all faithfull, and of all that *of Christ*
beleeue, *what it is.*

beleeue, wherefoeuer they be, whofe head is Chriſt himſelfe.

Ephe. 1.
Coloſſ. 2.

In Chriſtes bodie there is moꝛe fleſhe than bones, that is ſay, there be moꝛe weake in the faith, then there be ſtrong.

The body alſo of Chriſt, is the Sacrament of thankes giuing after a certaine manner.

To eate the fleſh and drinke the bloode of Chriſte what it is.
Ioan. 8.
1. Cor. 10.

What is to eate the fleſhe, and drinke the blood of Chriſt? It is to beleeue that Chriſt ſuffred his paſſion foꝛ our ſinnes. Al the Patriarkes and Prophetes beleeued in Chriſte, and Abꝛaham (as Chriſte ſaith) ſaw his day and did reioyce in it. &c. And they alſo did eate the fleſhe & dꝛinke the blood of Chriſt ſpiritually.

Virgine.

What is a Virgin? In Scripture it ſignifieth any honeſt faithfull woman, oꝛ the ſpouſe of Chriſt. Which ſpouſe is eyther any ſoule beleeuing in Chriſt, and liuing honeſtly, accoꝛding to his woꝛd: oꝛ els the whole congregacion and Church of the faithfull.

Harlot, or whore.

What is an harlotte, or whore? It is the vnfaithfull ſoule (whether it be man oꝛ woman) which ſeeketh health otherwhere than of Chriſt, apoſtaſing and running a-
away

way from Gods word and faith in Christ, vnto mans traditions.

False doctrine, and mans reason, be oftentimes called of the Prophets, whores and harlots.

Besides these, a whore or harlot signifieth a woman which committeth adulterie with another man.

What is vertue? A firme readinesse of *Vertue.* the wyll to goodnesse, ingendred by the worde of God : and made easie by oft and great exercise in doing well.

The morall vertues, and the outwarde fulfilling of the lawe, be also ingendred and gotten, by often exercising them. Some define them thus : saying that vertue is the meane betweene two excesses, whiche excesses bee called vices. Otherwhiles the fruites of the spirite in Scripture be called vertues.

And here ye must note, that all vertues consist in the deede and doing of them, as we read : The kingdome of God standeth not in wordes, but in power, effect, and doing of it. 1. Cor. 4.

Whas is vice? The fruite and worke of *Vice.* our corrupt nature, & the old man, & a readinesse

Rom. 7.
Iac. 2.

dinesse of the will to naughtinesse. There dwelleth not in me (that is to saye, in my flesh) ought that is good. Wherfore what soeuer is in vs that is good, commeth of GOD.

Sacra-
mentes
what they
are.

What be Sacraments and Signes? Good assurances and confirmations of the word of God.

Gen.3.9.17.

Some define them thus: Sacramentes be signes and witnesses of the will of god towardes vs, by whiche hee moueth and stirreth our heartes to beleeue. Such were the skinnes wherwith God clothed Adam and Eua, the Rainebowe, Circumcision, &c. Such be with vs, Baptisme, and the Sacrament of Christes bodie and bloude.

Baptisme.

What is Baptisme? The dipping into ẏ water, in token of repentance, and new-nesse of life to followe . It is also defined

Tit. 3.

to be the badge and cognizaunce whereby not onely we be knowen to be of the flocke of Christ, but that also wee bee stablished in our conscience, that we be in the fauor of God, and our sinnes forgiuen . It is called the cleane and pure water, the la-uacre of our regeneration, or fountayne of the newe birth.

What

What is the Sacrament of Christes bodie The sup-
and bloude, or of thankesgiuing? An holy per of the
mysterie of the bodie and bloude of Christ, Lorde.
institute of Christ, to be eaten of all Christian men, in token of remission of sinnes
through Christ: That euen as sure as we
take the bread, and eate it with the mouth
of the bodie, and drinke the wine: so verily
and certainly euē at the same instant, with
the mouth of our faith, we receyue the ue-
rie bodie and bloude of Christe, and there
it doth as actually comforte and suftayne
the soule, as dothe the breade and the
wyne nourishe and comfort the heart, and
the outwarde man.

And as verily as the most souereign pla-
ster and salue layde to a wounde or sore,
draweth oute the filth, and healeth it: so
verily and really doth the bodie and bloud
of Christe thus receyued, put awaye the
sores and deformities of the soule, and not
alonely maketh it whole, but also pure,
cleane, without scar, wrinkle, and spot, and
so maketh it a delectable, louely, and fayre
spouse in the sight of God. Lo what it is
to receyue the bodie and bloude of Christ
in faith.

What

Repentance.

What is penitence or repentance? We reade of two manner of kindes of repentances. One was a Legale in the olde lawe vsed of the Iewes and Israelites, This kinde of repentaunce is a certaine contricion of the minde, and hatred and detestation of our sinne, with a sorowe and compunction of the hart, which springeth and ryseth as soone as we begin to feele and perceyue the abhomination of oure sinne, by laping our deedes and desires of our heart to Gods lawe. Suche was the repentaunce and penitence of the Niniuets, and of Manasses, and of other, which were greatly sorie and compunct in their hart, what by considering their offences on one part, & the anger & iust wrath of God hanging ouer their heade for these offences.

Jonas. 3.
2. Par. 33.

The signes of repentance.

The tokens and outward signes of which repentaunce amongest the Iewes, was commonly clothing in sacke cloth, sprinkling and casting asshes vpon theyr heare, and fasting a day, two or three. This kinde of penitence may also the wicked men haue. For Iudas that betrayed Christ, afterward when he perceyued how wic-

Math. 27.

wickedly he had done, toke such care, sorowe, and pensifnesse, that for pure an-
guish he hanged himself. So horrible and
dreadfull were in his sight hell gates, the
wages & payment of his iniquity. There
is also an euangelicall penitence: whiche
is a continuall study, purpose, and ende-
uerment, and wilsull meditacion of morti-
fieng our fleshe, and fashioning our liues
to the wyll of the Lorde.

And this kind of penitence is onely in
them that are renued, and vnto whom the
forgiuenesse of sin through Christ is giue.

As for this word penaunce, because the
Popes clergy hath iugled with it so craf-
tely, and deceyued the poore innocentes
eyes, it is well done to reproue the euill
vse and handling of it, as the mainteyning
of the same is wicked.

What signifie the latter times in Scrip- *The latter*
ture? The Prophetes signifie by them *tims what*
commonly the dayes wherein the prophe- *they sig-*
sies, and the figures of the olde testament *nifie.*
going on Christ, toke effecte, and were
perfourmed. For when Christ came, both
the prophesies & figures ceased. And euer
sence, Christ is openly sincerely, clearely,

and

and without all shadowes set out and preached, and so shall continue vnto the worldes ende.

1. Timo .4.
1. Cor. 10.

Paule calleth The latter dayes, ŷ time a little before the end of the worlde, and the day of the iudgement of the Lord. In which we be euen nowe.

The ende
of the
worlde.

What is the consummation and ende of the worlde? It is when the state and forme of the worlde shall passe by. And when this chaunge of Winter, Sommer, and spring shall cease: when there shall be neyther night nor day.

The day
of the
Lorde.

Math. 25.

What is the day of the Lorde? The greate assemblement, court and parliament of all men that hath ben from Adam to the last man: at what day our Lorde Iesus Christ shall come with great power and maiesty and pronounce the last sentence and dome, both to the good, and to the euill, adiudging the euill to euerlasting punishment with the deuilles, and graunting the good and godly man euerlasting ioye and felicitie: to the which that we may come, God through our Sauiour Iesus Christ graunt, to whome be all honor and prayse. Amen.

Geue the glory to G O D alone.

¶ *An other booke of De-*
maundes of holy Scriptures : verye
profitable to all Students of
Diuinitie.

WHO is the author and maker of the most beautifull frame of this world? God: whiche by his almightie power, wisedom, and goodnesse, doth now also order, gouerne, and preserue the same.

Gene. 1.
Iere. 10,
Eccle. 18.
Act. 4.

What is God? An endlesse vncreated substance, without both beginning and ending : Which by his worde alone first created all things, and nowe disposeth and ruleth, yea, and conserueth all things: one substance distinguished, but not deuided into thre sundrie persons, the Father, the Sonne, and the holy Ghost, and notwithstanding remayning one alone, true, and perfect God.

Ioan. 1.

Math. 3.28.
1. Ioan. 5.

What is his word, whereby he first created, and nowe preserueth and gouerneth all things? It is the decreed sentence, appointment, will, power, and wisedome of

Ioan. 1.

Psalm. 41.

E.i.   God,

Eccle. 40.
Esay. 55.
1. Pet. 2.
Psalm. 119.
Ioan. 10.
Psalm. 80.
2. Thess. 2.
Ioan. 6.
Math. 13.
Gen. 2.
Sap. 2.
Eccle. 15.
Gen. 3.
Rom. 5.
Rom. 14.

God. The Sonne is also called the word, bicause he is the wisedome and might of his father, the word in the Scripture is oftentimes called by a metaphore, or similitude, water, wine, milke, a lantern or candle, the voyce of the shepeheard, the ryght hand of the Lord, the breath of the Lords mouthe, the bread of life, a pearle or precious stone, and such like.

In what state did God create man? Perfect, righteous, and good according to his owne image and likenesse: hauing fier and water set before him to take which he would, being endued with free will to doo euill, or to continue still in goodnesse,

What then condemned vs? Sinne by the lawe.

What is Sinne? Sinne is the transgression, or breaking of the whole lawe, or of any one commaundement of God. And all that is done without fayth, is sinne: and therefore the good workes of the infidelles doe nothing profite them.

What is the Lawe? A learning teaching vs with authoritie what ought to be done or auoyded, in thought, worde, or deede, with rewardes and punishmentes

Gal. 3.
Ephe. 2.
Ioan. 1.

for

for doing or omitting the same. This law is our schoolemaister to teach vs the waye to Christ, by whome the violence, sting, power, and the shadowes of the lawe bee take away: in whose place he hath brought in grace and truth.

Howe chaunced we to synne? By the choyce of our free will, graunted to vs either to doe good or euill: whereby we lost both our felicitie that we were first placed in, and that our free will also. Eccle. 15.

Howe then were both we and our forefathers reconciled to the fauour of God, which wee lost by our disobedience, being as vnfruitefull branches of the rotten roote of Adam? By the performance of the mercifull promise of God giuen to Adam, that the seede of the woman shoulde breake the serpents heade: Renued to Abraham, that in his seede all Nations shoulde bee blessed: and perfourmed by Christ, which by his death payd our raunsome: whiche promise and perfourmaunce conueyed vnto our forefathers and vs, and vnto all the Church by faith, hath ben and is the common and general meane of saluacion: they (that is to say, our forefathers) beleeuing Rom. 4. Gen. 3. 1. Timo. 2.

that

that Christ was to come by whome alone they should be saued: & we with no doubt-full faith confessing that he is come, dyed and rose againe for to regenerate vs to God, to mortify vs to sinne, the fleshe and the world, to rayse vp againe at the laste day, and so to take vs vnto him selfe, pla-cing vs in the glory of his father.

1. Pet. 2.

Who receyueth this benefyte? The church of Christ only.

What is the church of Christ? The whole number of the faithfull beleeuers in Christes comming, sufferance and resur-rection: members of the misticall body of Christ, Graines to make one loafe, Graps to make one wine, liuely stones to buylde on a spirituall house, in Christ to offer spi-rituall sacrifices acceptable to God tho-rowe the same Christ Iesus, which is the head of the saide body, the corner stone of the sayd house, the Lord and husband to the sayd church his spouse maried to him by faith.

1. Pet. 2.
Ephe. 1. 5.
Coloss. 2.
Psalm. 118.
Ose. 2.

Ioan. 1.

Who bestoweth this benefyte vpon vs? God through Iesus Christ his sonne, by whome he hath made vs his children also and fellowe heyres with Christe of hys glorie.

Galat. 3.
Rom. 8.

What sygnifyeth this name IESVS?
A Sauiour, which is the chiefe poynt of Math. 1.
his office, and cause of his comming into
this worlde, as appeareth by the wordes
of the Aungell to Ioseph, shee (meaning
Marie) shall bring forth a sonne, and thou
shalt call his name Iesus : For he shall
saue his people from their sinnes.

What signifyeth this name CHRIST? Christ is.
Annointed whereupon it may be gathered our king.
that our Sauiour Christ is a king, a priest Heb. 2.
and a Prophet, which . iii. were accusto-
med by the lawe ceremonial to be annointed. A king, bicause by inheritance he being the sonne of God, ought to be Lord,
and Ruler of all thinges, and bicause he
hath conquered and subdued vnto him selfe
by death, by bearing our sinnes, by redee-
ming vs his inheritance out of the power
of the deuill, all the whole kingdome, power and aucthority ouer death sinne and the
deuill. A priest bicause he once for all hath
entred *In Sancta Sanctorum* into the most
holy and innermost tabernacle of God, and Christ is
hath offered once for all a perpetuall suffi- our priest.
cient sacrifice to satisfy for al mens sinnes, Heb. 7. 9. 10.
and to purchase all mens redemption, net
E.iii.   ceasing

ceasing nowe still to be a perpetuall Medi-
atoz and Intercessoz to God his father, foz
man, he himselfe being both God and
man, making an ende of, and abolishing
all sacrifices and ceremonies, which were
but shadowes and significations to put
the Iewes in remembzaunce of his comming befoze he came. A pzophet, foz the
true and onely sufficient doctrine whiche
he pzeached being here in earth, and lefte
behinde him, wzitten by his Apostles foz
our learning, binding our conscience to be
subiect to none other doctrine, but to his
alone.

*Christ is
our Pro-
phet.*

By his kingdome hee hath made vs
kings, and heires of his kingdome by a-
doption, and conquerozs thzough his most
valiant victozie of oure enimies, sinne,
death, hell, and the deuill.

1. Pet. 2.
Apoc. 1.
1. Cor. 15.
1. Pet. 2.
Heb. 13.
Rom. 12.

By his Pziesthoode, with the holy oyle
of his spirite he hath made and annoynted
vs Pziestes, to offer to God the father
acceptable sacrifices thozowe him, whiche
are ŷ sacrifices of righteousnes, of pzaise,
of thankesgiuing, of an humble and contrite heart, of fayth, and wholye to cruci-
fie and offer vp our selues vnto him: and
by

by the same office, we being made partakers by him of the same, maye be bolde to come to the light of God, to offer vp our sacrifice and prayer.

By the office of his prophecie or scholemaistership, he doth lighten vs with the true knowledge of his Father, instructeth vs in the truth, and maketh vs the Disciples of God. By this annoyntment receyueth he these three offices to communicate them with vs, wherevpon we are called Christians.

What is a King? A rightfull magistrate, or heade power vnder God among men, ordeyned of God for the defence of the good, and keeping downe of the euill, according to right and iustice. Rom. 13. 1. Pet. 2.

What is a Priest? An officer appointed and licenced of God, to presente himselfe to the light of God, for to obtaine his fauour by intercession, or to pacifie his wrath by offring vp of sacrifice acceptable to him. Heb. 5.

What is a Prophet? A messenger of God, to declare the will of God, eyther in shewing the threatenings, or opening the promises, or expounding and declaring

E.iiii.   the

the mysteries conteyned in his holy worde or will to vs his children.

*Why doest thou call vs his children, see-*ing that Christ is his only son? We are not by nature the childre of god, as Christ only is, but by adoption & grace, or fauour of God. As for Christe he is of the same substance and essence with his father.

Christe by nature is the sonne of God, we by adoption.

By what meanes doe wee receyue at the hande of God these heauenly treasures: Or by what meanes are they conueyed vnto vs? By Faith.

What is Faith? An assured confidence and trust in the truth of God, in the merites and promises of Christ, conceyued thorowe Christ, by hearing of his worde, hoping still for the performaunce of the sayde promises, in the meane season not ydle, but still working by charitie: Or as S. Paule defineth it in his Epistle to the Hebrues: Faith is a sure confidence of things that are hoped for, and a certainty of things that are not seene.

Rom. 10.

Heb. 2.

What is Hope? A constant looking for of those things, which we haue conceyued thorowe faith by the worde of God.

What is Charitie? A godly vertue, a
louely

louely and gentle affection of the minde, whereby we loue God aboue all thinges, and our neighbour as our selfe. Charitie also is taken for the fruites of faith, and workes of mercie. Math. 25.

Who is my neighbour? Any man, vpon whome I doo execute the workes of mercy, or that standeth in neede of my helpe. Luke. 10.

Were we predestinate by the grace of God through Christ to this vocation, election, iustification, and saluation before the beginning of the world. Yea verely: so sayth S. Paule, he chosed vs in Christ Iesu before the foundacions of the world were layde. Agayne he sayth: we know, that al thinges worke for the best vnto them that loue God, which also are called of purpose. For those which he knewe before, he also ordayned before, that they should be like fashioned vnto the shape of his Sonne, that he might be the first begotten sonne among many brethren. Moreouer, whome he appoynted before them also he called. And whome he hath called, them also he iustified: & whom he iustified, them he also glorified. Ephe. 2. Rom. 8.

What is the grace of God? Gods fauour, beneuolence, and kinde minde, that of him Ephe. 2.

him selfe without our deseruing he beareth toward vs , wheréby he was moued to bestow vpon vs his Sonne Christ, and all other his good giftes, with free imputacion of his goodnesse, and vndeserued remission of our sinnes.

What is Predestinacion? The secrete vnchaungeable appointment of God before all beginninges by his counsell and wisedome to life euerlasting concerning his elect and chosen people : or any other beginning, ordering, or ending of all things.

Math. 11.

What is vocation? To be called of the Lord to any manner of benefite, office, or ministracion. There be two kindes of vocation: generall, as thus in S. Mathewes Gospell : come vnto me all ye that laboure and are laden, and I will refreshe you. Particular, as the calling or appointment of Kinges, Prophetes, Apostles, &c.

What is election? The choyce or appoyntment of God to anye ministration, office, dignitie, or preheminence, whiche immediatly followeth the particular calling, as for an example : He that heareth

Math. 22.

the word, is called : but he that beleeueth, is chosen. By this hearing and beleeuing

may

may this place be expounded: Manye are called, but fewe chosen.

What is Iustification? Of vnrighteous to be made righteous by the rigteousnesse of Christ, which we conceyue by fayth.

What is Saluation? To enioye the felicitie prepared of Christ for the faythfull: to be of the number of the glorified saints.

Whereby art thou certified of this liberalitie, and of these benefites of God towarde mankinde? By the office of the Apostles and Preachers appointed for the same purpose.

What is the office of the Apostles and Preachers? To preach the worde of God, or the Gospell of Christ, and to minister the sacraments, which Christ himself hath ordeyned to be vsed in the Church.   Math. 28. Marc. 16. 1. Cor. 4.

Howe is that proued? Christ sayd to his Apostles: go and teache all nations, baptizing them in the name of the Father, and of the Sonne, and of the holy Ghost. Againe: Go throughout the whole world, and preache the Gospell to euerye creature. And of the Supper of the Lorde, Christ sayde: Doe this in the remembraunce of me.   Math. 28. Mar. 16. Math. 26.

What

What is the Gospell? It is a doctrine conteyning the promise of free remission of sinnes purchased by Christ alone.

What is a Sacrament? A visible signe of an inuisible grace: or an outwarde element or corporall substaunce, appointed of God to certifie our fayth, wherewith onely wee receyue it, of the promises of God annexed therevnto.

Of howe manye partes doth a Sacrament consyst? Of two partes: that is to saye, of the element and of the worde.

Howe manye Sacramentes are there? Two: Baptisme, and the Lordes supper.

What is Baptisme? The washing of euerye beleeuing Christian in water, that taketh vppon him to professe the name of Christ, whiche water certifieth our fayth of the inwarde washing and clensing of our soules by the spirite of God: a token of our regeneration, of the mortification of our flesshe, of our buriall with Christe, and of our resurrection vnto a newe lyfe.

If the beleeuing Christians onely be baptised, according to this saying of Christe: He that beleeueth and is baptised, shall bee
saued:

1. Pet. 3.
Tit. 3.
Ioan. 3.
Rom. 6.

Mark. 16.

faued : *Why shoulde the Infantes be baptised, which for imperfection of age are not
able to beleeue ?* Though Infantes haue
not power to beleeue, or to confesse their
beliefe, yet haue they fayth imputed vnto
them for the promise sake of God, bicause
they bee the seede of the faythfull, as hee
sayde to Abraham: I will be thy God, and
the God of thy seede. Seeing then that
they also haue ý promise of saluation, why
should they be forbidde ý promised pledge,
or seale of ý same promised saluation : The
Sacramentes of the Iewes differd nothing
from ours in effect, but onelye in the outwarde element, and forme of executing the
same. Why then shoulde oure Infants be
more forbidden Baptisme, than the Iewes
infantes were forbidden Circumcision at
the eyght daye : Seing we reade that the
Apostles baptised sundrie housholdes, as
of Stephana, Lidia, Onesiphorus. ɣc. (if
a man may gesse at a thing, whereof wee
haue no certaintie) it is lyke inoughe, that
they baptised some Infantes also. But to
leaue all gesses and vncertain coniectures,
we are sure, that the Iewes infantes pas-
sed with their parentes out of Egypt thorowe

Gen. 17.

Gen. 17.

1. Cor.1.
Act. 16.
2.Tim.1.4.

Exod.13.14.

1. Cor. 10. row the red sea, and vnder the cloud, which were tokens of our baptisme.

What if the infants die, before they receaue the Sacrament of Baptisme? Gods promise of saluacion vnto them is not for default of ye Sacrament, minished or made vayne, and of no effect. For the spirite is Gen. 17. not so bound to the water, that it can not worke his office, where the water wanteth, or that it of necessitie must alway be there, where the water is sprinckled. Simon MaAct. 8.gus had the Sacramental water, but he had not holy Ghost, being in dede an Hipocrit and filthy dissembler. In the Chronicle of Act. 10. the Apostles Actes we reade, that while Peter preached, the holy Ghost came vpon them that heard him, yea and that before they were baptised: by the reason whereof Peter brast out into these wordes, & saide: can any man forbyd water, that these should not be baptised, which haue receaued the holy Ghost, as well as we? True Christians, whether they be old or young, are not saued bicause outwardly they bee washed with the Sacramentall water, but bicause they be Gods children by election through Christ, yea and that before the foundacions

of

of the world were layd, and are sealed vp by the spirite of God vnto euerlasting life, the giftes and calling of God being such, that it can not repent him of them. Notwithstanding, the Sacrament of Baptisme ought not therefore to be neglected, but with all reuerence to be embraced both of old and young. For he that despiseth the Sacrament, despiseth not the Sacrament only, but the authour of the Sacrament, which is Christ Iesus the Lorde.

Ephe. 2.
Rom. 11.

Note wel.

What is the Supper of the Lord, or the Sacrament of the body and blood of Christ? Bread and Wine consecrated, that is to say, made and appoynted of God to bee a Sacrament to put vs in rememberance, that as the bread is broken, and the wine powred out: so Christes body was broken, and his blood shed for our redemption. And as the bread receaued through our mouth, and digested in our stomacke, driueth away our hunger, and norysheth our body: the wine likewise receiued and digested quencheth our thirst, and quickeneth our bloud: so Christes bodie and bloude recepued by fayth, digested with worthie continuaunce therein, not disagreeing from the right recey=

receyuing thereof, slaketh our hunger and
thirst, that is to saye, our emptynesse of
grace, and dzynesse of fayth, nourysheth
and quickeneth both our bodye and soule,
making vs partakers of the whole merites
and dignitie of the bodie and bloude of
Chzist. And as the bzead of many granes
is made one loafe, and the wyne pzessed
togither of sundzy grapes : so wee being
many, are one body in Chzist: And bicause
we are of his body, we must needes also be
quickened by his bloude, and lyue of hys
spirite.

2. Cor. 10.

*Remayneth there the substance of breade
and wine after the wordes of confecration
(as they terme them) or but the accidentes
of them onely, as the authors of Transub-
stantiation haue heretofore taught?* If the
substaunce of bzeade and wyne shoulde bee
denied to remayne in the Sacrament of
the bodie and bloude of Chzist: so shoulde
it cease to be a Sacrament. Foz euery sacrament, as we haue tofoze hearde, consisteth of the wozd, and of the element. Now
yf we take away water from Baptisme, so
is there no Sacrament : verely euen so in
like manner take away Bzead and Wine
from

from the Lordes Supper, so ceaseth it to
be a sacrament. To declare that bread remayneth after the wordes of consecration, Saint Paule calleth it breade diuers times, as we may see in his first E-
pistle to the Corinthians. S. Luke also in
his Chronicle of the Apostles actes, whe-
soeuer he maketh mention of the Lordes
Supper, calleth it ẏ breaking of breade.
And it is to bee thought that so worthye
learned men woulde haue presumed to
call so honourable a mysterie, breade, if
there had bene no breade remayning, but
onelye the accidentes of breade, as oure
Transsubstantiators teache: Doth not
our Sauiour Christe after the wordes of
consecration call the misterie of his bloud,
the fruite of the vine: And who is so farre
estraunged from the right rul e of reason,
whiche knoweth not that the fruite of the
vine is wyne: Here doth it euidently appeare by the authoritie of Gods worde,
that in the Sacrament of Christes bodie
and bloude, there remayneth after the
wordes of consecration, the substance both
of breade and wine: whereof it truly followeth, that the Popishe doctrine of Trans-

1. Cor. 10.
11.
Act. 2. 20.

Matth. 26.
Marc. 14.
Luke. 22.

F.i.   substan-

substantiation is nothing else than a vaine
dreame and foolishe fancie brought in by
Antichrist, neuer knowne of ye ancient fathers of Christes church, nor yet receyued
of the Greekes vnto this day.

*Why sayst thou there but two Sacramentes, when we haue heretofore bene taught,
that there are seauen Sacramentes?* Because Christ in the newe Testament lefte
no mo to be occupied in his Churche. As
there were giuen to the people of the olde
lawe but two Sacramentes: That is to
say, Circumcision, and the Passeouer: so
likewise in the newe Testament. Christe
appointed but two Sacraments: that is,
in steade of Circumcision, Baptisme: and
in the place of the Passeouer, the Lordes
Supper. Therefore as for the rest, they
be not aptly called Sacraments. They be
honest trades, godlye orders of lyfe, and
vertuous, meete to bee exercised of Christians, as Matrimonie, Order, Penance,
Confirmation, and extreme vnction.

What is Matrimonie? A lawfull ioyning togither of one man and one woman
to liue chastlye togither, forsaking all other, for to bring forth children in the
feare

Gen. 2.
Math. 19.
1. Cor. 7.

feare of God, and to auoyde fornication, contayning an vnseparable fellowſhip of lyfe togither.

What is Order? Order hathe bene wrongfully taken both for a Sacrament, and for the annoynted order of Prieſthode, which Chriſt tooke awaye. But in deede, a godly, holy, and reuerende ſtate of Miniſters, Preachers, Paſtors, or Apoſtles, is of Chriſt allowed in the newe Teſtament, to be louingly and reuerently receyued of vs, as ſhepeheardes of the flocke. Of whome ſayeth Saint Paule : They that rule well, are worthie of double honour, but namely they that laboure in worde and doctrine.

1. Tim. 5.

What is Confirmation? A godlye allowance by the Biſhop or Preacher, of the children when they came to age, into the congregation of Chriſt, as a due examination or triall of their continuance in the ſame fayth, whiche their Godfathers or ſureties in their name profeſſed and promiſed for them at their Baptiſme to kepe. And this Confirmation is as it were a diſcharge of the Godfathers bondes.

What is penaunce, or repentaunce? A

F.ii.   ſorow

sorow conceyued by the feeling of the lawe in the hart or conscience because of sinne, without desperation, ioyned with a ful determined purpose to amende, which commeth not of the lawe, but of the grace of God. This penaunce or repentaunce consisteth of contrition, faith, confession and correction.

What is contrition? A Passion or griefe of the conscience, which it suffreth by the mouing and pricking of the lawe, wee being not able to fulfill it. This contrition is an acceptable sacrifice to God, as Dauid saith: a contrite and humble hart, O God, thou wilt not despise.

Psalm. 51.

What is faith? A sure perswasion of enioying the benefites, which God the father hath moste mercifully promised for Christes sake to all sinners without exception, that repent in faith.

What is confession? An humble acknowledging of our sinnes to God, hoping for forgiuenesse: to man, seeking for good counsell and helpe of prayer: not denying them or stoutly standing to the defence of them, but humbly submitting our selues to the mercy of God.

What

What is correction? An amendement of our former euill life, taming of our carnall wyll : mortifyeng of our flesh : applying of our selues to the commaundement, wyll and example of Christ : to take away and banish the euill : to bring in and establishe the good, as Dauid sayth : eschewe euyll and doo good. Psalm. 34. 1. Pet. 3.

What is extreme vnction? Extreme vnctiō ought to be the preaching of the word of God to be declared to the pacient by the spirituall minister. And to this preaching ought praiers also for the sick to be ioined. As touching þ annoynting of the sick with oyle, it is but a Iewishe custome, whereunto the true Christians are not bounde. The Minister outwardly annoynteth the paciente with the mercifull promises of God. God inwardlye annoynteth him with his holy spirite, whereby he is comforted and made strong, bothe paciently and thankfully to beare his crosse, to call vpon the name of God, and in all poyntes to giue himselfe ouer to the blessed will of God without any resistance. Iac. 5.

Well, thou hast hitherto declared the great kindenesse of God towarde vs : tell me Of our duty toward GOD.

nowe, what is our dutie towarde him. To loue him, feare him, honour him, followe him, serue him, beleeue in him, to fight vnder his standarde with all fayth, charitie, truth, despising of worldlye things, thanksgiuing, innocencie, fasting, prayer, obedience, humilitie, and pacience, to put of the olde man, and to doe on the newe, to denie our selues, to take the Crosse vpon vs : to forsake all that wee haue for his sake, and to set forth the glorie of his name, that we maye become a worthie Temple for the holye ghost, and meete heyres for the kingdome of heauen, the true land of promise flowing with milke and honie.

What is it to loue God ? To cast oure whole minde and affection vppon God with all reuerence, and earnestly desire to followe his will.

What is it to feare God ? The feare of the Lorde is a lyke reuerence as children owe to their parents : a willing and faithfull heede, that wee committe nothing against him or his worde, that we offende not so louing a Father, but rather diligently apply our selues to liue according
to

to his commaundement, alway thinking that God doth presently see and beholde all our deedes, words, yea, and thoughts. This feare is the beginning of wisedome. This feare maketh him blessed that hath it. This feare is the fountayne of life. This feare keepeth vs from sinne. And besides a number of other commodities, this feare maketh vs more warely to take heede of the craft of Satan. The feare of the Lorde is also taken for the worshipping of the Lorde, as it is written: They feare mee in vayne with the commaundementes of men. Ionas the Prophet also sayde : I am an Hebrue, and feare the God of heauen.

Prou. 1.
Eccle. 25.
Pro. 14.
Eccle. 1.
Esay. 29.
Ionas. 1.

If these manye profites and commodities come of the feare of God: howe chaunceth it that the deuilles doe not enioye the same, which feare the Lorde as much as we? As much in deede, but not as well. For there be two kindes of feare : A childishe or reuerent feare, whereof I haue alreadye spoken : and a seruile, bonde , or slauishe feare . The feare of the vngodlye. by the consideration of the lawe, and feare of punishment, as likewise is the feare of the

Iac. 2.

Two kinds of feare.

deuils,

deuils, is bonde, seruile, and thrall. Of
this feare speaketh Saint John in hys
Epistle, on this maner: Feare is not in
charitie, but perfect charitie casteth feare
out of the doores. This feare is called a
mightie feare in the Psalme, bicause all
things by it are done in vnfaythfulnesse,
in such ignorance and lacke of knowledge
of the mercie of God, as thoughe God
were no naturall fatherly God, but a seuere narrowe eyed Judge, or cruell ty-
rant. These two kindes of feare are well
described of the Poet Horace on this maner:

1. Iom. 4.

Psalm. 90.

> *Oderunt peccare boni virtutis amore:*
> *Oderunt peccare mali formidine pœnæ.*

Which may thus be translated into En-
glishe:

> *Good men doe well of a vertuous entent:*
> *Euill men do well for feare of punishmēt.*

What is it to honour and worship God?
Both with our whole mynde and strength
thereof, and with the bodie and power
thereof, as subiect to the mynde, and both
to God, to reuerence and prayse God, to
to declare our loue and feare towardes
                                     him.

him.

What is it to followe God? To beleeue in him, to keepe his doctrine and obey it, to follow him whithersoeuer he leadeth or calleth vs, to beare what burden soeuer he layeth vpon vs, to doe as he hath done before vs, and giuen vs an example to doe after him.

What is it to serue God? To liue according to his word, to beleeue in him, to referre all thinges to his glorye, to helpe our neighbour, to obey him as our Lorde and maister, whose seruice is no bondage but freedome, whose burden is light, whose yoke is pleasant, as Christ sayth: take my yoke vpon you, and learne of me: for I am meeke and lowly in hart, and ye shall finde rest to your soules. For my yoke is easye, and my burden is light. Saint John also saith: his commaundements are not greuous.

Math. 11.
1. Ioan. 5.

What is it to beleeue in God? To receaue his seede and doctrine into our hart: to commit our selues wholely vnto him in all thinges, and certainely to assure our selues that all thinges are true, and shall vndoubtedly be performed, which he hath promised.

mised.

What is it to fight vnder his standarde?
To followe the example of our captaine
Christ. As he by death hath conquered sin,
death, hell, and the deuill: so we by morti-
fiing of our flesh ought to suppresse, subdue,
and conquer the same, with the helpe of our
sauiour and captaine, whose standarde the
crosse vnles we follow, we perishe and become a praye to our enemies, neuer to bee
redemed, yf he doe not raunsome vs.

What is truth?   Christ him selfe the
word of God , and what soeuer agreeth
with him, which can neyther deceaue, nor
be deceaued. I am the way, the truthe, and
the life, sayth Christ . And in his prayer to
God the father he sayth: thy worde is the
truth. The ciuill truth is an agreemente of
wordes and deedes, to say as the thing is,
and as we know it to be , Of this truthe
speaketh the Apostle in his Epistle to the
Ephesians, saying : put away lying, and
speake euery man truth vnto his neighbour, forasmuch as we are members one of
an other. Also the Prophet Zacharie: speak
euery man the truth to his neighbour: let
none of you imagine euill in his hart a-
gainst

Ioan. 14.
Ioan. 17.

Ephe. 4.

Zach. 8.

gainst his neighbour, and loue no false
othes.&c.

What is it to despise worldly thinges?
Wholly to set our minde vppon heauenly
thinges, not regarding the transitorie and
vncertaine vanities of this world, according to the wordes of S. Peter: all fleshe
is as the grasse, and all glory of man as
the floure of the grasse, &c. Knowing and
acknowledging with S. Paule, that wee
haue here no certaine abyding place, but
seeke for one to come: againe, that as we
brought nothing into the world, so shall we
cary nothing out of it: but hauing meate,
drinke, and cloth, we ought to be content
and abundantly satisfied, forasmuch as
godlynesse is great riches: yf a man be
content with that he hath.

What is thankesgiuing to God? To remember the benefites of the Lord, confessing and acknowledging also come of him,
ottryng him our whole hart, loue & seruice
for the same.

What is innocencie? A mind or confer-
ence gyltie of no sinne, which commeth
through faith in Iesus Christ, as the Apostle sayth: we being iustified by faith, are

at

I. Per. I.
Esay. 40.
Iac. I.
Heb. I3.

1.Tim.6.

Rom. 5.

at peace with God, through our Lord Jesus Christ: by whome also it chaunced vnto vs to be brought in through fayth vnto this grace, wherein we stand, and reioyce in the hope of the glory of God.

What is fasting? To beware that wee oppresse not the bodie, and so by that meanes the minde also, with surfetting, drunkennesse, and excesse, as our Saviour

Luke. 21.

Christ sayth: Take heede to your selues, least at any time your hearts be overcome with surfetting, & drunkennesse, & cares of this lyfe, &c. Agayne, to liue chastly, purely, and soberly: to abstayne from vices, to bring oure bodie into bondage to the spirite, and the spirite to God: to minister to the bodie only ꝩ that is necessarie, to mortifie the flesh with the affections and lustes of the same. The right abstinence from meates taken as a way or helpe to the abstinence from sinne, consisteth not in the qualitie, but in the quantitie of ꝩ meat, not what, but how much meat & drink thou receyuest. For whether fasteth more aright, he that moderately receyueth of flesh, or he ꝩ cloyeth himselfe with fish? All things are pure to them ꝩ are pure, sayth the Apostle.

I.

All

All the creatures of God are good, and no=
thing to bee refuſed, if it be receiued with
thankeſgiuing. For it is ſanctiſied by the
worde of God and prayer.

Why then is this lawe ſo earneſtlye eſta=
bliſhed with ſuch penaltie vpon it, that wee
eate no fleſhe on Fridayes, or other dayes ap=
pointed to abſtayne from the ſame? I take
that as a ciuile poſitiue Lawe, lyke to the
actes of Parliament, made for ſundrie and
diuers purpoſes concerning the ſtate of a
Realme, and for the wealth of the ſame.
For if it were anye lawe of God binding
our conſcience, no King nor Pope myght
diſpence with the breaking of it.

What is prayer? To call vpon the name
of the Lorde, aſſuredly truſting to obtayne
that we require, ſo that wee aſke of him in
his ſones name and none other, that thing
whiche he will to bee required and none o=
ther, that eyther for obtayning of good
things, auoyding of euill, or releaſing and
forgiueneſſe of euill and ſinnes paſt. What
ſoeuer ye aſke in my name, ſayeth Chriſt= Ioan. 14.
that will I doe, that the Father maye bee
gloriſied by the Sonne: If ye ſhall aſke a=
ny thing in my name, I will do it. Againe
veri=

Ioan. 16.

verilye, verilye, I say vnto you: Whatsoeuer ye shall aske the Father in my name,
he will giue it you. And Saynt Iohn in

1. Ioan. 5.

his Epistle sayth : This is the truste that
we haue in him, that if we aske any thing
accordyng to his will, he heareth vs. And
if we knowe that he heareth vs, we knowe
that we haue the petitions that wee desire
of him.

What is obedience ? A lowlye and hartie submission of our selues to God, and af-
terwarde to oure Parentes, to the Magi-
strates, to oure Superiours, and to all
those, to whome God hath committed the
rule and gouernance of his flocke and people in this worlde, or in iust causes, to all
them, to whome we be by anye title inferiour.

*But what yf our Superiours wyll enforce
vs to obey them in vniust causes ?* In this
behalfe we owe them no obedience. God is
the highest Magistrate. If any inferiour
Magistrate commaundeth any thing, con-
trary to his godly commaundement and
blessed wyll, we must aunswere with the a-
postles. *Oportet deo magis obedire quam
hominibus,* We must obey God more then
men.

Act. 5.

men. Examples hereof we haue many and diuers both in the olde and in the newe Testament.

What is humilitie? A subiection of the proud hauty courage of our mind, shewing our selues inferior to all men, presuming in nothing, esteming our selues worse then all men in our owne conceates. And this is that, which the apostle saith. In gi- Rom. 12 uing honor goe one before an other. A-gaine, be not hye minded, but make your selues equall to them of the lower sorte. Be not wyse in your owne conceates. Hereto agreeth the saying of S. Peter: submit your selues euery man one to an other. Knit your selues togeather in lowlynesse of mind. For God resisteth the proud, and 1. Pet. 5. giueth grace to the humble. Submit your selues therefore vnder the mighty hand of God, that he may exalt you when the time is come.

What is pacience? Willingly without resistance eyther in thought word or deede to suffer vndeserued punishment after the example of Christ, which prayed for them Luke. 23. that persecuted and moste cruelly tormen-ted him. This pacience is described of S.

Peter

¶ Pet. 2.

Peter in his first Epistle, where he sayth: seruauntes, obey your maisters with feare, not only yf they be good and courteous, but also though they be froward . For this is thanke worthy , yf a man for conscience toward God endure griefe , and suffer wrong vndeserued . For what prayse is it, yf when ye be buffeted for your faultes , ye take it paciently . But and yf when ye doo well , ye suffer wrong, and take it pacient= ly , then is there thanke with God . For hereunto verely were ye called: for Christe also suffered for vs, leauing vs an example, that we should follow his steppes, whiche did no sinne, neyther was there guile found in his mouth: which when he was reuiled, reuiled not againe : when he suffred , he threatned not, but committed ẏ vengeance to him that iudgeth righteously. &c.

What is the olde man , that we must put of ? The naughty , corrupt , and rotten nature, which sithens the fall of Adam we haue lineally at our first generation recea= ued of our parentes through the corrupti= on of the first roote Adam . Or thus: the noughty concupiscence , lust to sinne, and affection of our fleshe, without faith, of this

olde

olde man speaketh our Sauiour Christ on
this maner: That which is borne of flesh Ioan. 3.
is fleshe. And except a man be borne from
aboue, he cannot see the kingdome of god.
Also the Apostle: Laye from you the olde Ephe. 4.
man, which is corrupt according to the
deceauable lustes. Againe, put of the olde Coloss. 3.
man with his workes.

*What is the newe man, that we must doo
on?* The renewyng of man by fayth and
the word of God: the spirite of God geuen by Christ our spirituall and second A-
dam: Agayne, to tame the old man our
fleshely and first Father Adam: to beget
vs agayne and adopte vs to God, whiche
Spirite we receaue by Christ at our regeneration. Of this newe man speaketh
our Sauiour Christe thus: That whiche Ioan. 3.
is borne of the spirite, is spirite. Also S.
Paule: Be renued in the spirit of your
minde, and put on the newe man, whiche
after God is shapen in righteousnesse Ephe. 4.
and true holynesse. Againe: put on the Coloss. 3.
newe man, which is renued in the knowledge and image of him that made him.

What is it to denye our selues? Playnly to professe, that all our laboures and

workes

workes profit nothing vnto saluatiō: to slea the old Adam with al his lusts & affectiōs.

What is it to forsake all that we haue for Christes sake? To esteeme al that we haue not to be ours for his sake, and willingly (if neede so require) for the professiō of his name to depart from wyfe, children, parentes, freendes, countrey, house, landes, and all thinges els that we doo or may enioye, yea and to put our selues in danger of all perill for the name of Christ, and profession of the Gospell. He that loueth father or mother more then me (saith Christ) is not worthy of me. And he that loueth sonne or daughter more then mee, is not worthy of me. And he that taketh not his crosse and followeth me, is not worthy of me. He that findeth his life, shall lose it: and he that loseth his life for my sake, shall finde it. Agayne, if a man come to me, and hate not his father and mother, and wyfe and children, and bretheren or sisters, yea & his owne life also: he cannot be my disciple. And whosoeuer doth not beare his crosse, and come after me he cannot be my disciple.

Math. 10.

Luke. 14.

What is the crosse, that we must take vp-
on

on vs? Any soꝛow oꝛ payne that belong=
geth to any vocation oꝛ trade of life foꝛ the
tryall and pꝛofe of our faith and pacience.
Also it is the coꝛrection, chaſtening rodde
and ſtaffe of the Loꝛd, wherewith he puni=
ſheth them, whome he loueth, not to theyꝛ
damnation oꝛ vtter caſting away from his
fauour, but to ſaluation, and to teach vs to
flyꝛ vnto him in oꝛr trouble ⁊ aduerſity, as
childꝛen to our moſt deare ⁊ louing father.

*What is ment by the name of the Lorde
whoſe glory we muſt ſet forth?* The glo=
ry, pꝛayſe, wyſedome, might, power, woꝛ=
ſhip, honoꝛ and maieſtie of the Loꝛde. Oꝛ
the knowledg, pꝛeaching and aduauncé=
ment of his holy woꝛde.

What is the temple of the holy Ghoſt?
An honeſt, godly, and faithfull chꝛiſtian
hart, in the which God is rightly woꝛſhip=
ped in ſpirite and truth: wherein are offe=
red ſpirituall ſacrifices of pꝛayſe, innocen=
cie, thankes geuing, of an humble and con=
trite hart, whoſe chiefe coꝛner ſtone is
Chꝛiſt. Knowe ye not, ſaith Saint Paule,
that ye are the temple of God, and howe
the ſpirite of God dwelleth in you: If a=
ny man defile the temple of God, him ſhall

Ioan. 4.

1. Cor. 3.

G.ii.   God

God destroye. For the temple of God is holy, which temple ye are. Saint Peter also sayth: Ye as liuing stones are made a spirituall house, an holy Priesthode, for to offer vp spirituall sacrifices, acceptable to God by Iesus Christ.

What is the kingdome of heauen? The kingdome of heauen is diuerslye taken in the Scriptures. First, for the holy Gospell and worde of God, because that is the scepter and yron rodde, whereby God ruleth, reygneth, and dwelleth in the hearts of the faythfull. Of this kingdome speaketh Christ in the Gospell on this wise: I will giue thee the keyes of the kingdome of heauen, that is to saye: I will commit vnto thee the office to preache the Gospell of saluation, which openeth and vnlocketh vnto men the waye and doore, by the whiche they may be saued, and enter into the kingdome of heauen. Item, the kingdome of heauen is lyke vnto leauen, which a woman tooke and hydde in three peckes of meale, tyll it were all leauenned.

Secondlye, the kingdome of heauen is taken for fayth it selfe, as Saint Paule sayeth:

Margin notes:
1. Pet. 2.
Math. 16.
Math. 13.
Rom. 14.

sayeth : The kingdome of heauen is not meate and drinke, but righteousnesse, and peace, and ioye in the holy ghost.

Thirdlye, the kingdome of heauen is expounded the whole congregation of the faythfull abyding in this lyfe, in whome the Lorde by his worde and spirite, doth inuisibly dwell and reygne. Of this kingdome speaketh Christ in the Gospell on this maner: The kingdome of heauen is Math. 25 lyke to ten virgines, whiche tooke their lampes and went to meete the Brydegrome. Fyue of them were wyse, and fiue were foolishe. &c.

Fourthlye, the kingdome of heauen is taken for the ioye, felicitie, and pleasure, which the soules of the beleeuers enioye, when they are departed out of this world: and their bodies also ioyned with the soules at the day of Iudgement shall enioy, euen in that place, which Christ hath prepared for them to possesse : where they shall bee comforted with the sight of his Maiestie and Godheade, and with the fruition of his perpetuall felicitie with him . Of this kingdome speaketh Christ in the Gospell: When ye shall see Abraham,

Luk. 13. ham; Jsaac, and Jacob, and the Prophets, in the kingdome of God, and you to bee driuen out of the dores.

Finallye, the kingdome of heauen is wheresoeuer Gods worde is preached: from which kingdome they onely are excluded, whiche beleeue not the worde, according to this saying of Christ: He that is of God, heareth the wordes of God. But yee heare not, bicause yee are not of God. Agayne, My sheepe heare my voyce. Item, Euerye one that is of the truth, heareth my voyce.

Ioan. 8.
Ioan. 10.
Ioan. 19.

What meanest thou, by a lande that floweth with milke and honie? Pleasaunt, abundance of all things, both sweete and profitable. By the honie is vnderstoode sweetenesse, ioy, gladnesse, and pleasure. By the milke, pure nourishment, whereby we still continue, growe, and increase in fayth and godlynesse vnto the measure of Christ.

When shall we enter vppon, and enioye this kingdome, this promised lande, that floweth with milke and honie? The church militant in this worlde, gouerned by the spirite of their most mightie, valiant, victorious,

torious, and triumphant Captayne
Christ already enioyeth after a certayne
maner in spirite, thorowe fayth in this
kingdome and blessed lande, as it is written : He that beleeueth on the Sonne, Ioan. 3.
hath euerlasting life : Hee that beleeueth
not on the Sonne, shall not see lyfe, but
the wrath of God abydeth vpon him. But
when they are ioyned togither both bodie
and soule with the reast of the faithfull
congregation, which are departed out of
this world in the faith of Christ, to make
one whole tryumphant congregation,
when they haue by the power of Christe
conquered the malignant church of the deuill, which shall be at the last day of iudgement, which we doo dayly looke for nowe
in these latter times : then shall they true-
ly and perfectly enioye and possesse all the
ioyes and pleasures of that most ioiful and
pleasant lande : whereof Dauid speaketh Psalm. 27.
on this manner : I beleeue to see the good
things of the Lorde in the land of the liuing. Nowe we see in a glasse, sayth the
Apostle, euen in a darke speaking : but 1. Cor. 13.
then shall we see face to face. And as S.
John saith : It dooth not yet appeare

what

what we shall be . But we knowe , that
when it shall appeare, we shall be like him.
For we shall see him , as he is . The eye
hath not scene, and ý eare hath not heard,
neyther haue entred into the hart of man
the thinges, which God hath prepared for
them that loue him. And all these thinges
shall the elect congregation of God enioy
and possesse immediatly after the ende of
these latter times wherein we now liue.

What callest thou the latter times? The
first times were vnder the lawe of nature,
till the lawe of Moyses . The seconde vnder the lawe of Moses, till (the kingdome
thereof abolished) Christ entred into this
worlde. Nowe the thirde and last time is,
and hath bene , sithence the entring of
Christ into this worlde, to take our fleshe
vpon him , by ioyning in him togither
both Godheade and Manheade with an
vnseparable knotte to reconcile and knitte
togeather God and man, nowe that all the
prophecies & figures of Christ be brought
to an ende . The last times also are the
times, that goe immediatly before the day
of the Lord, and ende of the world . Saint
John saith : Little children , it is the last
time.

Marginal notes:
1. Ioan. 3.
1. Cor. 7.
1. Ioan 2.

tme. Saint Paul saith : We are they, whom the endes of the world are come vp-on. Saint Iames saith : The comming of the Lorde draweth nigh . The Iudge standeth before the doore. And our Sauiour Christ himselfe say̅h : The time is at hande. Beholde, I come shortly, and my rewarde is with me, to giue euerye man according as his deedes shall be. 1. Cor. 10 Iac. 5.

Apoc. 22

Howe farre thinkest thou that daye to be hence ? No man can pronounce any cer-taintie of the time, when that day shall be, as our sauiour Christ sayth : Of that day and houre knoweth no man, no not the Aungels in heauen, but my father onely. Agayne : It is not for you to knowe the times and seasons, which the father hath put in his owne power. Saint Paule saith that the day of the Lorde shall come euen as a thiefe in the night . For when they shall saye : Peace, peace, all things are safe : then shall sodayne destruction come vpon them (as sorowe commeth vppon a woman trauayling with childe) and they shal not scape. Notwithstanding although the holy Scriptures doe passe ouer with silence the certaintie of the time when

Math. 24.

Act. 1.

1. Thess. 5.

Christ

Christ shall come to iudge the worlde, as
a thing more curious than profitable for
our saluation, that by this meanes wee
might set our selues in the more readinesse
against his comming, bicause we are not
certaine of the day and houre: yet we may
plainely perceyue, that it is not farre of,
both by the comparison of our dayes with
the dayes of Noe (For thus saith Christ
as it happened in the dayes of Noe: so shal
it be also in the dayes of the Sonne of
man. They did eate and drinke: they maryed wyues and were maryed euen vnto
the same day that Noe went into the
Arke: and the floud came and destroyed
them all. &c. Euen so shall it bee in the
day, when the sonne of man shal appeare)
and by the shortening of the dayes promised in the Scripture for the electes sake,
and diuers other argumentes besides.
Nowe when that day shall once come,
(which vndoubtedly shall come out of
hand) then shall the Lord seperate the
Sheepe from the Goates, rewarde the
vngodly with punishment due to their vn-
beleife: and the godly he shall put in pos-
session of that most glorious and blessed
kingdome

(marginal notes:)
Math. 24.

Luk. 17.

Math. 24.

Math. 25.

kingdome, whiche he purchaſed for them by the crucifying of his bodie, and ſhedding of his bloude. To this Lorde Chriſt, our alone Sauiour, with the Father and the holy Ghoſt, be all honour and prayſe, both now and euer. Amen.

Giue the glorie to God alone.

¶ To the Christian Reader.

Upon vewe of these our demaunds, Christian reader, if thou further demaunde some question of the boke, of the towne for which it is, of the Author, and of the Printer, no answere I suppose so fully iust (be it that the question double it self twice and againe) as to adiudge the one both in name and deede holy, the other in life godly, the third in his worke learned, the last in his intent carefull for them, and not vnmindefull of thee. For in whatsoever true religion, christian example, godly inuention, and studious enterprise coulde be beneficiall, in that haue they all ioyntly, and seuerally eche, by doctrine, practise, wit, with paynfull and no lesse chargeable endeuour, serued, if not satisfied thy godly contentation. And for that in doctrine, all thinges are written for instruction, rightly to vnderstande, faithfully to beleeue, and readily to confesse that reason of hope which we haue, demaunde who will frende or aduersarie, aunswere who shall skilfull or vnlearned: to eche of these Christian dueties, with respect of their person,

*son, and eche capacitie, this little Pamphlet
ministreth readilye sufficient furniture by
playne explication of the principall grounds
of our religion, worthy of thy diligence, thou
if not vnworthy of the knowledge. But I la-
ment with alas. What is it to talke rightly
or smothly, and to walke crookedly? Is not
the sweete Christian harmonie in consent of
saying and doing? For what discorde maketh eyther of these by it selfe, or what a-
greement? To apply or pleade very olde and
almost deade example, hath some force to
vice or vertue, in priuate talke or publike
sermon. And the late allegations of Fraunce
or Flaunders, purporting noueltie, doe spe-
dily quicken our dull sense of hearing: but
the home made mention of our familiars,
whose affection doth it not moue to eyther
side? What can you more greedily heare, or
I long, as with child, to tel. The great grace
and gift of God on Sandwich towne, by the
sound of the Gospel, hath it wrought in vain
with the townesmen? are they taught wel, &
not wel gouerned? shew thei forth gods prais
with mouth, and plucke it down with hand?
or rather they expresse their fayth by their
works, and their works by faith, in brotherly
loue,*

loue eche to other, in liberalitie to the poore,
in hospitalitie to the Straunger, in erection
and maintenance of schooles, in most carefull prouision that no one among them lyue
ydle. Which godly proceedings, when the
father of this booke, that painfull and godly instrument of Christ his church, maister
Thomas Becon did with priuate comforte
beholde, he coulde not with safe dutie but
acknowledge & soūd out the same publikly,
to the great prayse of God, the increase of
their beginnings, and example of all others,
who by reason of decay through sande and
shelf albeit they cannot so happily ēter their
welnere stopped hauen, yet by view of their
race in Iesus Christ, maye finishe the same
course by repayred lyfe to their hoped heauen. And therefore this worke he tooke in
hande, in order and matter excellent, edify-
ing by question, playne for capacitie, and
briefe for memorie, not as the Seraphicall
and Sorbonicall Doctors of the schole, who
giue sucklings in religion vinegar for milk,
the stronger hard stones for hartie meat: but
following the precept of Saint Paule, teacheth and confirmeth them in such as bee
good and profitable. But least the author of

his

To the Reader.

his intent, the Senate and towne of Sandwich of their benefite shoulde be frustrate,
and the commendation of their godly example hidden from such as coutende to followe,
wee haue thought it good nowe first sepa-
rately and alone to print the same, whiche
before, without greater charge in buying
the whole workes of Thomas Becon, coulde
not be had. This our labour if thou shalte
accept, it cannot be otherwise, God giuing
grace, but that in all profitable maner wee
shall be further carefull and diligent
for thy Christian vtili-
tie. Farewell in
Christ.

R. D.